Challenges for Business
in the 1970's

Challenges for Business in the 1970's

By the Editors of *Fortune*

Little, Brown and Company — Boston - Toronto

LIBRARY OF CONGRESS CATALOG CARD NO. 73–183853

FIRST EDITION

T 06/72

Published simultaneously in Canada
by Little, Brown & Company (Canada) Limited

PRINTED IN THE UNITED STATES OF AMERICA

Contents

Introduction

This is a book about the U.S. economy during the next decade, and its aim is to help readers think about the kind of economic growth we are likely to be experiencing in the decade. In a sense, however, the book is not about economics at all. It is concerned primarily with events and trends of a kind that economists call "exogenous." The word, admittedly not very lovely, has been turning up more and more in discussions of our economic future (and is not altogether avoided in these pages). It refers to events that are external to the economy but that may nevertheless impinge on and drastically reshape it.

The distinction between events that are exogenous and events that are truly economic may seem, at first glance, a bit esoteric. But consider what is involved. Ordinarily, anyone trying to estimate the dimensions and character of future economic growth looks at certain kinds of data: about the size and composition of the labor force, the availability of money and credit, physical capacity in different industries, the trend of productivity, and so on. It has always been understood that noneconomic events, and especially wars, may invalidate any analysis based on these data; on the other hand, it has been presumed that there are few such noneconomic events and that they are relatively infrequent. In other words, it has been presumed that the background against which economic changes take place is relatively stable.

It is this presumption that has come to seem outdated in the last few years. Beginning in the mid- to late 1960's, we have been increasingly bothered by a sense that the background no longer looks stable. Our basic institutions are under attack; our traditional values are suddenly in question. The rules of the game are changing; and the result is that anyone trying to forecast the outcome of the game is beset by entirely new kinds of uncertainties.

Take, for example, the massive new problems involved in making a forecast about the economy's growth rate — a kind of forecast that was difficult enough in any era. Traditionally, economists began the exercise by examining the expected growth rates of the labor force (this could to some extent be inferred from the age composition of the existing population) and the trend of productivity gains. If economists expected the labor force to grow by 1 percent a year and productivity to grow by 3 percent, then they could calculate that the economy had a growth potential of 4 percent a year. The labor force might, of course, grow more or less rapidly than expected, or its growth might be offset by reductions in average hours worked (there never was an "age of certainty" in economics); still, one knew at least what the basic elements of the calculation would be.

Today the basic elements look blurry, and our notions about the future size of the labor force, and the trend of productivity, are in disarray. Large numbers of young people seem to be attracted by a hedonistic "antiwork" ethic. They have drifted off into the drug culture, or gone to live in communes, or dropped out in some other way; and if they are in the labor force at all, they don't look very productive. At the same time, large numbers of educated young women have indicated that they are determined to do more advanced and productive work than such women have done in the past. Meantime, many young men and women have suggested that they have very selective notions about the kinds of companies and industries they are willing to work for; many seem to gravitate to public-service jobs whose contributions to the economy may be marginal (their contributions to society may be more substantial).

And the new uncertainties do not end with the changing career preferences of young Americans. Quite a few Americans of all ages are now persuaded that threats to the environment should dictate a considerable slowdown in economic growth in the years ahead. The economic goals that we once took for granted — full employment and maximum economic growth — are suddenly in question.

Thus the largest questions confronting anyone who is concerned with the economy's future are about "the background." As the author of the first chapter observes, "The most interesting questions about the economy these days . . . are noneconomic questions."

The book is based on a series of eight articles in *Fortune*, the last of which appeared in the August 1971 issue. The basic conception of the series owes a great deal to Sanford S. Parker, the head of *Fortune*'s economics department; and the department itself helped the authors of the series at numerous points. The first chapter, defining the new age of uncertainty, was written by Charles E. Silberman, who also helped to develop the conception of the series and to establish the subjects it should emphasize. In addition, Mr. Silberman wrote chapter 3, on the new consumer markets. Lawrence A. Mayer is the author of chapter 2, which deals with new uncertainties about population trends, and chapter 6, on the new outlook for capital goods. Chapter 4 (the auto market) was written by Dan Cordtz, chapter 5 (the military-space "market") by Gilbert Burck, chapter 7 (the economics of environmental control) by Gene Bylinsky, and chapter 8 (new directions in government) by Max Ways.

The book also owes a great deal to the *Fortune* researchers who helped to prepare the original magazine articles. These were, in order: Marjorie Jack, Marilyn Wellemeyer, Lorraine Carson, Ann Tyler, Jeanne Krause, Varian Knisely, Ann Hengstenberg and Sally Shaver. The charts used throughout the book were done by, or under the supervision of, Alexander Semenoick of *Fortune*'s art staff.

In preparing the book, *Fortune* was assisted by many businessmen, government officials, academic specialists, and other "sources." We owe a substantial debt to them all, and regret that they are too numerous to be mentioned by name here.

THE EDITORS OF *Fortune*

One

The U.S. Economy
in an Age of Uncertainty

Unprecedented social, political, and psychological uncertainties will affect growth prospects for the Seventies. The difference between high and low projections works out to an incredible $500 billion in 1980 G.N.P.

As we move into the decade of the Seventies, we have the greatest opportunity for progress at home of any people in world history," Richard M. Nixon told Congress in his 1970 State of the Union message. "Our gross national product will increase by 500 billion dollars in the next ten years, This increase alone is greater than the entire growth of the American economy from 1790 to 1950. *The critical question is not whether we will grow, but how we will use that growth.*" (Emphasis added.)

Nixon's formulation represents a radical shift in presidential perspective. Throughout most of the postwar period the critical question was precisely the one that is now being taken for granted: whether the economy would — whether it *could* — keep growing rapidly enough to keep the labor force fully employed. Not that economists or government officials have been uninterested in the uses to which economic growth might or should be put. The allocation of resources between the defense and nondefense sectors, the relative priorities to be attached to private and public spending, and the distribution of income have all been subjects of controversy and concern in past years. But the central issue — it was, for example, the principal domestic issue in Richard Nixon's and John F. Kennedy's 1960 presidential campaign — has been how to achieve economic growth.

The new tendency to take it for granted is a byproduct of the superboom of the 1960's, the longest period of uninterrupted economic growth in this century. To be sure, the growth has stopped, in part as a result of the Administration's attempt to halt inflation, and Nixon and his economic and political advisers are very much concerned with getting the economy moving upward again. But even with the present short-run difficulties, there is a clear tendency to take long-term growth for granted. The tendency draws strength from the uniform optimism of the forecasts of the economy of the 1970's that have been published in the last several years. The U.S. Bureau of Labor Statistics, the Council of Economic Advisers, and the National Goals Research Staff, and private organizations such as the National Industrial Conference Board, the National Planning Association, and McGraw-Hill have all published forecasts that output will grow about as rapidly in the Seventies as it did in the Sixties.

A breakdown of the trends

Between 1959 and 1969, real gross national product increased by an average of 4.3 percent a year. Among the more highly publicized forecasts of the 1970's, the most pessimistic calls for a growth rate of 4.1 percent a year; most of the forecasters put the growth rate at about 4.3 percent. If realized, these confident projections would mean a 1980 G.N.P. approaching $1.5 trillion, in dollars of 1970 purchasing power.

The confidence may be entirely misplaced.

Under ordinary circumstances, extrapolating past trends may be a reasonable enough way of projecting the future. But these are not ordinary circumstances. Since 1966, for example, the two critical components of growth — increases in productivity and in the labor force — on which all the forecasts ultimately rest have departed widely from their long-term trends. Since 1966, productivity growth in the private economy has averaged only about 1.6 percent a year, only half the long-term trend of 3 to 3.2 percent. The labor force, on the other hand, has shot up by more than 2 percent a year since 1965, a third higher than its long-term trend.

To be sure, long-term trends are not scripts to be followed without any departure; both G.N.P. and its components fluctuate somewhat above or below their trend lines from year to year. But when the basic components depart so widely from their long-

term trends for so long a period, it seems reasonable to inquire
about the trends themselves.

The new interesting questions

The turmoil and tension of the last half dozen years represent a
special reason for being wary of these trends. Indeed, given this
turmoil, and the uncertainty it has evoked about the stability —
at times, even the viability — of the American polity, there is
something almost fatuous about predicting the course of the
economy over the next decade with the certainty that a single
projection implies. Certainly the greatest need so far as both
businessmen and economists are concerned is to reexamine the
political, social, cultural, and technological as well as economic
forces that underlie, and ultimately determine the validity of,
any projections. The most interesting questions about the economy these days are, in fact, noneconomic questions.

Lest there be any doubt, it should be understood that *Fortune*
is not taking a turn toward pessimism; it is quite possible that
the standard forecast of 4.1 to 4.3 percent a year growth in
G.N.P. during the Seventies will turn out to be too low rather
than too high. The point is not that the outlook has become
gloomy but that it has become uncertain. There is, in fact, more
uncertainty about the probable course of the economy over the
next ten years than there was at the beginning of either of the
two preceding decades — uncertainty over both the size of the
economy and its composition.

We begin with uncertainties about the extent to which political, social, cultural, demographic, and technological change may
affect the rate of growth of the nation's labor force and its
productivity. If the slowdown in productivity were to continue
while the growth in the labor force fell back to "normal," the
rate of growth in the nation's productive capacity, and hence in
G.N.P., could be as little as 2.5 percent a year or thereabouts.
This sounds like an incredibly low figure in the wake of the
superboom, yet it was in fact the average of the Eisenhower

years. The growth rate could be even lower if, for example, labor-force growth, compensating for its recent sharp increases, fell *below* the so-called norm.

But the growth rate might be far higher than is now expected. If, for example, productivity were to regain the momentum of the early Sixties and the labor force continued to grow at the rate of the last several years, real G.N.P. might actually grow at an average of 5.5 or even 6 percent over the next five to ten years.

The implications are staggering: these outer limits in the rate of economic growth could mean a difference of as much as $200 billion in the size of the gross national product in 1975 — i.e., a G.N.P. as low as $1,100 billion or as high as $1,300 billion, in dollars of 1970 purchasing power. By 1980 the difference between the high and low possibilities could reach $500 billion. The same basic uncertainties make it hard to get a line on the *composition* of the economy during the 1970's — i.e., on the market for such major components of G.N.P. as housing (and consequently appliances and home furnishings), automobiles (and consequently gasoline, steel, auto repairs and insurance, travel, and so on), electric power, clothing, recreation and capital goods.

Hence this new report on the U.S. economy in an age of uncertainty. This chapter will outline the potential impact on the economy of these new uncertainties. Subsequent chapters will focus on them individually.

The rise of exogenous forces

There is nothing new, to put it mildly, in uncertainty about the economy. How much consumers will spend on new clothing, cars, homes, or what have you, has always depended, especially in the short run, not only on current income and prices but on the degree of confidence consumers feel about future income, their expectations about price movements, their response to changes in styling and design, and their general mood.

Businessmen are equally prone to unpredictable behavior: how much they choose to invest in inventory and in new plant and equipment depends not only on consumer behavior but on the vagaries of "business confidence," which at times may bear only a tenuous relation to objective reality. Most major business decisions, John Maynard Keynes argued some thirty-five years ago, are taken "as a result of animal spirits — of a spontaneous urge to action rather than inaction, and not as the outcome of a weighted average of quantitative benefits multiplied by quantitative probabilities." The reason, Keynes suggested, is not that businessmen or consumers are irrational, only that "human decisions affecting the future . . . cannot depend on strict mathematical expectation, since the basis for making such calculations does not exist." Uncertainty, in short, breeds more uncertainty.

Economists find it useful to distinguish between uncertainties of this sort, which are in fact the raw material of the science of economics, and exogenous uncertainties, which have their origin in political, social, and cultural forces "outside" the economy. There is greater uncertainty about the long-term economic future now than during most of the postwar period, because these exogenous forces are so much more important now than then.

Until five or six years ago, for example, it seemed as though the U.S. had entered a golden age of stability. Sociologists proclaimed the end of ideology, and university professors pondered their students' political apathy; economists marveled at the spectacular expansion of the middle-income group and the apparent consequent erosion of class differences and conflicts; political scientists discoursed at length on the stability and viability of the two-party system; intellectuals from a number of academic disciplines developed the new science of "futurism," in the belief that stability made it possible to predict social, political, cultural, technological, and economic trends with a good deal of confidence; foreign educators admired our system of universal public schooling and mass higher education and tried to imitate it; foreign economists and businessmen envied the high and rising productivity of American workers and the efficiency of American corporate managers; and consumers everywhere sought to emulate American patterns of consumption. But whether one applauded or deplored American society and culture, its apparent stability and success meant that businessmen and economists could project and plan for the future with a high degree of confidence.

If Marshall McLuhan is right

Our uncertainties today begin with the possibility that Americans may be embracing a set of values so different that they add up to a whole new outlook on life and work and society. If the prophets of the new *Zeitgeist* are right — if seers like Marshall McLuhan, and Charles Reich are even remotely close to the mark — the new values could profoundly alter consumer demand, on the one hand, and the growth of productivity and the labor force, hence of the economy's capacity to produce, on the other.

What is the significance, for example, of the apparent weakening of "the Protestant ethic," with its emphasis on hard work, self-reliance, and self-denial, and the growth of new attitudes toward work and life? The attitudes have shown up in several different ways.

• There is the revolution in sex mores, or at the least, in attitudes toward sex — witness the transformation of the movies and of the legitimate theater.
• There is the growing emphasis on immediate rather than deferred gratification — both cause and effect of the "credit-card economy." Even the banks now advertise "Why wait?"
• There is the general questioning of authority, tradition, and custom, exemplified not just in the pervasiveness of protest and rebellion, but in increasingly casual (and usually more comfortable) modes of dress.
• Most important, perhaps, there is the growing search for meaning and purpose in our lives, the attempt to find some justification for activity in social and moral terms. The most interesting

manifestation of this, perhaps, is an apparent tendency — still small, but growing — for corporate managers, lawyers, and other professionals to seek purpose *outside* their job itself. While the number of college-age volunteers has dropped precipitously since the expansion of the Vietnam war, the Peace Corps is having increasing success in attracting engineers, lawyers, businessmen, and skilled craftsmen. Prestigious law firms in New York, Washington, Chicago, and elsewhere are finding that they can attract and hold many of the best young lawyers by giving them time, at company expense, to work on *pro bono publico* cases. And corporate presidents and chairmen increasingly seem to feel the need to justify business operations not in traditional profit terms but by referring to their corporate contribution to solving urban, racial, or environmental problems.

On a broader scale, the shift in values is manifest in the growing preoccupation with the quality of the physical environment and of life itself. "The time has come for a new quest," Nixon announced in his State of the Union message of January 22, 1970. "A quest not for a greater quantity of what we have — but for a new quality of life in America." Elsewhere in the same message, the President elaborated on the theme: "In the next ten years we shall increase our wealth by 50 percent. The profound question is — does this mean we will be 50 percent richer in a real sense, 50 percent better off, 50 percent happier? Or, does it mean that in the year 1980 the President, standing in this place, will look back on a decade in which 70 percent of our people lived in metropolitan areas choked by traffic, suffocated by smog, poisoned by water, deafened by noise and terrorized by crime?" And in September 1970, in a special message to Congress on his domestic legislative proposals, Nixon suggested that the title of the first report of the National Goals Research Staff — "Toward Balanced Growth: Quantity with Quality" — be the national theme for the 1970's.

We do not yet know how far these changes will go, how profoundly they will take hold, or what their economic implications will be. This is not the first time that a new order has been announced. "The dissolution of the ancestral order is still under way, and much of our current controversy is between those who hope to stay the dissolution and those who would like to hasten it," Walter Lippmann wrote in 1929, beginning a chapter entitled "The Breakdown of Authority" in his book, *A Preface to Morals.* (Some students of sexual behavior believe that there was a much more profound change in sexual mores in the 1920's than in the 1960's.)

It will be some time, therefore, before a definitive judgment can be made as to whether "the new values" represent a clear break with the past, or no more than a further (if perhaps accelerated) evolution of tendencies that have been evident for perhaps the last half century.

A new *Zeitgeist* might have even more serious implications for the supply side of the economy, particularly as it affects attitudes toward work and authority. As Tilford Gaines, vice president and economist of Manufacturers Hanover Trust, has written, "It was not coincidental" that the economic growth of the last century "first started in those countries where class systems were breaking down, where democratic political concepts were emerging, and where the dominant religious faith stressed self-reliance and hard work." Obviously, the growth of newer, more hedonistic attitudes toward work and life could adversely affect the growth of productivity and of the labor force.

At the same time, however, it should be recognized that the reverse is also possible   that Americans may want to work harder than ever. What Professor Zbigniew Brzezinski of Columbia University calls "the third American Revolution," which is moving the U.S. into the "technetronic era," or a "post-industrial society," is rapidly increasing the number of jobs that are themselves inherently interesting and rewarding.

Reasons for working hard

The change is just beginning, and "in the process," as Brzezinski writes, "it is creating three Americas in one. There is the emerging new America symbolized by the new complexes of learning, research, and development that link institutions of higher learning with society and create unprecedented opportunities for innovation and experimentation, in addition to sparking increased interest in the fine arts and culture." In this America, work tends to be synonymous with play; professionals work long and arduous hours without complaint. The second America — industrial America — is peopled by blue-collar and white-collar workers who on the one hand are "gradually forgetting the traumas of the Great Depression and beginning to enjoy both security and leisure," but who on the other hand are the fiercest opponents of the new hedonism. The third America is the pre-industrial America of sharecroppers, migrant farm workers, black "immigrants" to the big cities, miners in Appalachia — for the most part, men and women who want nothing quite so much as the opportunity to embrace the ethic of work, income, and consumption. In Brzezinski's vision of the future, all three Americas have reasons for working hard; if he is right, the result could be a rapid *acceleration* of productivity.

The rapid expansion of governmental intervention in the economy represents another major source of uncertainty. To be sure, governmental intervention per se is not new. What is changing is in part the scale of the intervention and, more important, an intrusion into areas that in the past had been largely or wholly private. Indeed, the growing preoccupation with the quality of life is introducing a whole new dimension of uncertainty into the American economy, for the general acceptance of the notion that we must reorder our priorities means the politicalization of some of the most important — and heretofore private — decisions about the allocation of resources. And quite apart from resource allocation, it could mean governmental action in areas — e.g., the birth rate, population distribution — that in the past were settled neither by the market nor by government.

The most visible expansion of government's role in the economy concerns the environment. If the national health requires a substantial reduction in air and water pollution, there is no practical alternative to governmental action of some sort; no one can buy his share of clean air or water in the open market.

The result is to create new uncertainties with which the usual economic forecasting techniques cannot cope. Take the auto market, for example. When *Fortune* published the series on "The Changing American Market" (1953–54) and "The Markets of the Sixties" (1959), it was possible to project the demand for new cars in a systematic way, putting together analyses of population trends (to estimate the potential number of "new," i.e. first-time, owners) with projections of consumer income, analyses of trends in scrappage rates, rates of growth in second- and third-car owners, and judgments about changes in automobile styling and consumer tastes. The projections necessarily contained a margin of error; in any short period car sales might run higher or lower as a result of changes in styling, credit terms and availability, consumer mood, and so on. But these year-to-year variations tended to cancel out one another, and over the longer term car sales conformed closely to the forecasts.

Newer forecasts are a much more doubtful proposition. It is still possible, of course, to project car sales on the traditional basis, and the governmental and private organizations that have published projections of the Seventies have done so. Their usefulness is questionable, however, in a decade in which non-market forces may be critical for both supply and demand. Certainly the auto market in 1975 or 1980 is likely to depend less on scrappage rates or trends in population and income distribution than on what Congress or the large cities do about air pollution. Of what use are existing projections if the federal government sets deadlines against auto-induced pollution? This is not a vague prospect; in December 1970 Congress passed amendments to the Clean Air Act which mandate a 90 percent reduction in certain forms of auto pollution in new cars by 1975. The important questions about the auto market, in short, are political (what are the probabilities of various mixes of governmental policy?), social (will Americans give up their love affair with the automobile in return for cleaner air?), medical (how much pollution can we stand?), and technological (what kinds of antipollution measures are possible over the next five and ten years, and at what costs?).

Concern about the environment creates equally large uncertainties for the electric-power industry. Electric utilities have been doubling their capacity every ten years, and most economists project that trend for the next two decades, at least. But any serious effort to reduce the enormous air and water pollution that is now a byproduct of electric-power generation could make it impossible for utilities to expand that rapidly. Public concern over pollution is already causing serious delays in construction of power plants in cities around the country, and in a number of instances has forced utilities to cut the size or change the location of projected plants.

Delays aside, measures to reduce pollution would substantially raise the cost of electricity, with as yet indeterminate consequences for individual households as well as industries like aluminum, steel, and paper, which use huge amounts of electric power. "It may be that energy consumption is growing so fast in part because the price does not include the full cost to society of producing and delivering it," Dr. Lee A. DuBridge, Nixon's former science adviser, suggested in testimony before a Senate committee in February 1970. He added: "I believe that efficient power production is just as important as ever to our economic growth, but we delude ourselves and perhaps short-change future generations when the price of electricity does not include the cost of the damaging impact its production imposes on the air, water, and land. If the total social cost of electricity or other products is included in its price, consumers will have the inherent ability to consider the effect of their decisions on the environment."

Concern over the environment is not the only reason that the government's economic role is expanding. The growth of "nonmarket public decision making," as sociologist Daniel Bell of Harvard calls it, is a matter of choice as well as of necessity. Federal subsidies for apartment rental or home purchase on the part of low- or middle-income families, federal actions to divert the flow of savings into home mortgages, federal subsidies to encourage private firms to develop new home-building technologies, a "national growth policy" to encourage development of "new towns" and older, smaller cities, federal subsidies to parochial schools and private colleges and universities, welfare reform to guarantee a uniform minimum income for the poor — these are of a different order from governmental action to clean up the environment. And Richard Nixon wants to go further in these directions than his Democratic predecessors.

When decisions are visible

Whatever the reasons, the effect of this growth of nonmarket public decision making is clear: the greater the number of economic decisions that are made by public agencies, the greater the potential for social and political conflict, and the larger the uncertainties about the size, and even more the composition, of the gross national product. The virtue of the market, as Professor Bell points out, is that it disperses responsibility. "When a 'decision' is reached by the multiple choices of thousands or millions of individual consumers acting independently in the market, there is no one person or group of persons to blame for such decisions. If a product 'does not sell' or there is a shift of taste, and firms or even entire industries fail because of such market decisions, no single group can be saddled with the charge of being responsible. But with nonmarket public decisions, the situation is entirely different. The decisions are visible, and one knows whom to blame." The result is to multiply the possibilities of community and group conflict.

Nonmarket decision making creates uncertainty not only because it increases the probabilities of conflict but also because it introduces a large element of discontinuity into business operations. Defense contractors, who depend on decisions made by government (and not on decisions made in the marketplace), have alternated between feast and famine for years; now civilian industries may face similar problems.

Another large source of uncertainty about the economy resides in the specter of social unrest and disorder. The U.S. has always been a violent society and, as the Eisenhower commission (the National Commission on the Causes and Prevention of Violence) pointed out, "The decade of the 1960's was considerably more violent than the several decades preceding it and ranks among the most violent in our history."

There is reason to fear that the Seventies might outstrip the Sixties in that regard. Racial violence, though it has somewhat abated recently, still has the potential to burn cities. Business has already had a taste of violence by Weathermen and other white radical groups. Witness the rash of arson and bombings in 1970 — the destruction of the Bank of America's branch in Isla Vista, California, the bombings of I.B.M., General Telephone, General Electric, and Mobil Oil offices in New York. Between January 1, 1969, and April 15, 1970, according to statistics collected by the Internal Revenue Service, there were 975 explosive bombings in the U.S., 3,355 incendiary bombings, and 35,129 bomb threats.

The economics of repression

Perhaps the greatest danger is that the threat of disorder and violence may provoke a wave of repression that could turn the U.S. into an armed camp. The possibility of social disorder or repression creates economic uncertainties of several sorts. The most talked about is a fear that racial conflict will make both whites and blacks reluctant to enter the downtown areas of large cities at night, or even during the day. If the fear is great enough, it could evoke a large-scale exodus, not only of department stores and other retail establishments, but of banks, insurance companies, and corporate headquarters. The greater danger is more subtle, involving the national psyche. Any extended period of social disorder or repression might erode an already weakened confidence in the nation's future. By destroying the "spontaneous optimism" on which borrowing, lending, and investment ultimately depend, disorder, or simply the fear of it, could seriously depress investment and, thereby, the over-all rate of growth.

Another uncertainty has come to seem larger in recent months. It lies in the possibility that, even with a somewhat controlled economy, the U.S. may be unable to halt inflation without sub-stantially more unemployment than the nation is willing to tol-erate. Recent studies by the Urban Institute and the Brookings Institution independently reached the conclusion that the "trade-off" between unemployment and inflation is a good deal less fa-vorable than most economists had previously thought. The Urban Institute study, for example, indicates that even with a 4 percent unemployment rate, the price level would rise by nearly 4.5 percent a year. It is possible, of course, that manpower train-ing programs and computerized job banks (to provide a better "fit" between job vacancies and available workers) could im-prove the trade-off; but efforts in this direction are still in too early a stage to permit easy optimism.

Most projections of aggregate G.N.P. these days are arrived at through a relatively simple technique. The essence of the tech-nique is to view total output as a function of (a) the number of workers, or, more precisely, the number of hours worked; and (b) productivity, i.e., the quantity of goods and services they produce.

How to think about the future

The first step in drawing up a long-term forecast of G.N.P., therefore, is to project the size of the labor force in the terminal year — in this case 1980 — and to convert it to an employment figure by making some assumption about the unemployment rate — usually 4 percent. This employment figure is then trans-formed into a projection of total man-hours worked by applying to it an assumption about the rate at which hours worked will decline. When the forecaster has a figure on the growth rate of hours worked, he then needs only a figure on the rate at which productivity will increase, on average, over the period at hand. By definition, the projected growth in man-hours plus the projected increase in output per man-hour adds up to the projected increase in total output, or G.N.P.

Given this technique, it is scarcely surprising that such disparate groups as the Conference Board and the Bureau of Labor Statistics have produced almost identical forecasts of 1980 G.N.P. The forecasts are similar because they are based upon similar assumptions about labor force and productivity. To judge the usefulness of these projections, therefore, we need to examine the factors affecting the growth of the labor force and productivity in more detail.

Take the detailed BLS projections of the labor force in 1980. Ordinarily, these projections are offered, and received, with a high degree of confidence; after all, people who will be working in the next ten years have already been born. And since immigration rates and death rates both tend to be quite stable, the only uncertainty comes from changes in what economists call "participation rates" — the proportion of various kinds of people actually seeking employment. Historically, changes in participation rates account for less than 10 percent of the change in the labor force (with population growth accounting for the rest).

Yet participation rates have not been behaving the way the projections say they should. Between 1960 and 1968, growth of the labor force averaged 1.6 percent a year, which is about what BLS had originally projected for the decade. Yet the accuracy of the projection is misleading: BLS was right because of two large offsetting errors. It had substantially underestimated the growth in the female labor force and, because of the impact of the Vietnam mobilization, overestimated the growth in the male labor force. Since 1965 the labor force has actually been growing by 2.1 percent a year, almost a third again as fast as its so-called trend. These facts by themselves would seem to raise some large uncertainty about the projections for the 1970's, which foresee the labor force growing by 1.7 percent a year.

The fact is that the seemingly dry data on participation rates are reflecting some fascinating recent changes in the character of

American society. Thus the entire difference between the actual and projected growth of the labor force in recent years is accounted for by the increase in the number of working women twenty and over. Most of this increase, moreover, reflects a tendency for more and more younger women to enter — or remain in — the labor force. It is not only that more married women now return to the labor force when their children are grown; more women with young children are also working now. And since women are marrying later and waiting longer to have the first child, those who do stop working during their child-rearing years nonetheless are in the labor force for a longer period of time.

It is probable that these tendencies will continue or even accelerate. They will certainly be encouraged by the "women's lib" movement. By producing a fundamental change in women's perception of their roles, and by opening up more intrinsically interesting jobs, the movement might increase the number of women who work for the satisfaction of the job as well as for income.

And yet it is also possible that these tendencies will be reversed (as the BLS projections implicitly assume). The largest uncertainty about them involves the *Zeitgeist*. If a new anti-work ethic takes hold, even the BLS projections of labor-force growth could prove too high.

But in the last analysis, the rate at which productivity grows will, more than anything else, determine the size of the markets of the 1970's. Over the postwar period, rising productivity has accounted for two-thirds to three-quarters of growth in total output. Thus the assumption forecasters make about the probable trend of productivity growth is central to their forecast of G.N.P. As with the labor force, recent experience casts a cloud over forecasters' tendency simply to extrapolate postwar trends into the future. As already noted, productivity in the private economy has been growing by only 1.6 percent a year, on average, since 1965 — about half the average of the postwar period.

The recent spurt in productivity lends some credence to the prevailing view that the earlier lag was no more than the usual top-of-the-boom phenomenon. But the recovery is still too brief and its course too uncertain to be sure of this view. The length and pervasiveness of that lag raise questions that cannot be dismissed easily.

The values of the young

Uncertainty about the future course of productivity growth stems, again, from questions about the *Zeitgeist*. It seems likely that any broad diffusion of basic new values would begin among younger workers. And as it happens, younger workers will be the major source of labor-force growth in the 1970's: Those aged twenty-five to thirty-four will increase by more than 50 percent. (Workers over forty-five will increase by only 4 percent.) They will also have considerably more education, on average, than the older age group. If Professor Brzezinski is correct in believing that Americans will want to work harder, the combination of demographic and attitudinal changes could provide a synergistic boost to productivity. But if McLuhan and Reich are correct, the fact that so large a proportion of the increase in the labor force will occur in the younger age groups could depress productivity.

Another source of uncertainty grows out of the relation between technology and productivity growth. Some economists expect the huge capital-goods boom of the Sixties to yield dividends in the form of accelerated productivity growth once the economy resumes its upward momentum. According to the "wringer hypothesis" of some BLS economists, business firms usually do not realize the full benefits of new or improved technology until they have been forced to go through the wringer, a process that leads them to cut costs and work at productivity gains.

But there is also a good bit of concern that a number of major industries may have exhausted the productivity gains from old technologies and have not yet developed new technologies. For example:

- Electric and gas utilities increased output per man-hour at an average rate of 6.2 percent a year between 1947 and 1965; since then the increase has averaged only about 4.1 percent. The reasons are not altogether clear; but some economists and engineers have suggested that the industry may have reached or passed the point of diminishing returns in its tendency to keep increasing the size of generating units. The problem is not so much that utilities can no longer realize economies of scale, but that concentrating output in fewer but bigger generators means huge productivity losses when one of the units breaks down. It also means increasing opposition to construction of new power plants from people in the area.

- In the communication industry, productivity has also been lagging, and H. I. Romnes, the chairman of A.T.&T., has expressed concern that future gains will be much harder to come by. Until recently, the gains have come in large measure from the steady conversion to dial telephones, i.e., from the application of technology developed at the turn of the century. These gains have now been exhausted, and the company has been forced both to increase total employment and to accept a lower level of experience among employees.

Another hypothesis about the productivity lag suggests that the decline of the Protestant ethic has affected corporate managers as well as workers. The point is not so much that managers work less, or less hard, than they used to, but that their motivation has changed — specifically, that more and more executives seem to feel the need to justify themselves by referring to the social ends that business serves, rather than to profit maximization. This change, Alan Greenspan, president of Townsend-Greenspan (and a Nixon economic adviser), suggests, has obvious implications for efficiency in business.

The rapid expansion of antipollution measures raises still another set of questions about productivity. Since the price system as now constituted does not reflect the costs of pollution, any significant attempt to reduce pollution means new inputs of capital and labor that will not be reflected in any increase in output. By definition, therefore, antipollution measures will tend to lower productivity. There may be powerful indirect effects as well. The electric-power industry, for example, is a major source of pollution; if more stringent regulations prevent utilities from expanding capacity in line with demand, power shortages could cut productivity in many manufacturing industries.

In the face of all these uncertainties, it seems quite foolhardy to attempt a single projection for the Seventies. In fact, not even *Fortune*'s upper and lower projections represent the outer limits of what seems entirely possible. Perhaps the economy will continue to operate and grow much as it has in the recent past. But looking ahead to 1980, all we can say is that any such "normal" growth is just one of a number of possibilities.

Two

New Questions about the U.S. Population

Will families get even smaller? Is a federal "population policy" emerging? What will the coming decline in teen-agers mean for U.S. society (and U.S. markets)? Will new living arrangements mean fewer "households"?

There are new problems, these days, in projecting the size and characteristics of the U.S. population. To be sure, demographers have had their troubles all along in projecting these matters. In the 1930's they generally anticipated a stable or declining population, and in the early 1960's, just before the growth rate fell sharply, many of them were looking ahead to explosive new growth. In the circumstances one might suppose that demographic projections are now worth very little. That is by no means the case. The new "age of uncertainty" has in some ways made demographic projections more interesting and more useful than ever. At the least, they serve to indicate just how wide the range of possibilities in the 1970's really is.

Behind the new uncertainties are some far-reaching changes in American life. People are embracing new values and seeking greater self-expression; social and moral standards are changing; many potential or long-dormant conflicts between social groups or classes — including those between women and men — have become overt; the government is intervening in the economy in new ways; and new concerns about the environment will also have an impact on the economy in ways that cannot be foreseen.

Most of the new questions about population growth have to do with pressures for slowing it down. Thus the big question today is not so much whether the trend to a slow growth rate will reverse itself but whether the rate, which declined through most of the 1960's, will decline still further. The final count for the census of 1970 showed a total of 205 million Americans, a gain of 25 million over 1960. A decade or so ago very few demographers guessed it would be that low: in 1960 the consensus choice among the available Bureau of the Census projections

How Many More Rich Americans?

The new uncertainties about the U.S. economy make it possible that economic growth between now and 1980 will be quite a lot lower — or higher — than the widely accepted standard forecast; and this implies a wide range of possibilities about the distribution of income at the end of the 1970's. In 1969, as the chart below shows, 18 percent of all family units (i.e., families plus individuals) received $15,000 or more before taxes. If real gross national product rises at the standard forecast rate of 4.3 percent annually, 40 percent could be in that class by 1980. If, however, G.N.P. advances at a sub-par 2.5 percent rate, only 25 percent will do that well. Should G.N.P. growth speed up to about 6 percent a year, 50 percent of all family units will be gettin

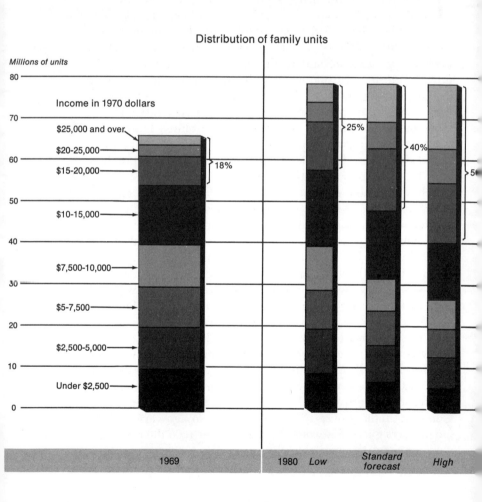

Distribution of family units

Millions of units

Income in 1970 dollars

$25,000 and over
$20-25,000
$15-20,000
$10-15,000
$7,500-10,000
$5-7,500
$2,500-5,000
Under $2,500

18%
25%
40%
5

1969

1980   Low   Standard   High
                forecast

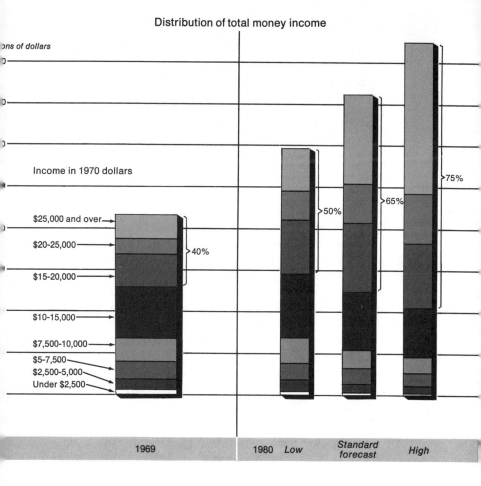

Distribution of total money income

ons of dollars

Income in 1970 dollars

$25,000 and over

$20-25,000

$15-20,000

$10-15,000

$7,500-10,000

$5-7,500
$2,500-5,000
Under $2,500

>40%

>50%

>65%

>75%

1969 | 1980 Low | Standard forecast | High

least $15,000. On these three assumptions, median income per unit would come to 0,000, $12,350, or $14,700. And on the high projection, more units would be in e $25,000-and-over bracket in 1980 than in the $10,000-to-$15,000. (All the figures in 1970 dollars.)

e last full year for which income figures are available is 1969. Between that year and 80, real income will rise about 70 percent if G.N.P. climbs at the standard 4.3 per- nt rate. It will increase only about 35 percent if G.N.P. should go up by 2.5 percent nually, but will nearly double if G.N.P. advances 6 per cent or so a year. The $15,000- d-over income group already receives about 40 percent of all money income; by 80 it will be getting from 50 to 75 percent of the total.

was a population increase of more than 30 million by 1970. The U.S. population grew by 13.7 percent in the 1960's, down from 18.7 percent in the 1950's.

If recent trends continue, the increase in the 1970's will be only about 22 million, or 11 percent. And it is easy to envisage even smaller figures. What is extraordinary about these modest forecasts is that they are being made at a time of rapid growth in the number of women in the prime ages of childbearing. In this decade the number of women aged eighteen to twenty-eight will increase from 17,800,000 to 22,400,000. Total births seem destined to increase until at least 1980, but the odds are against their reaching an annual level of five million even then.

Families have been getting smaller, and, obviously, many demographers expect young parents to continue to want smaller families than their predecessors. That this may indeed be the case is the conclusion of an exhaustive analysis of a nationwide survey financed by the federal government. The analysis suggests that families want an average of but 2.5 children. Furthermore, current data on births imply that some such average is about what women now in their childbearing years will end up with. Previous surveys have always arrived at a figure of three or a little higher. The difference works out to around 1,350,000 fewer births in 1980.

The road to ZPG

A number of reasons have been advanced for the trend to smaller families. One is the pill. Another is the rising cost of properly raising and educating children. Beyond these, concerns about pollution, the environment, and the possible overcrowding of parts of the U.S. have together somewhat tarnished the ideal of the immediate post-World War II families — a lot of children in an idyllic suburban location. The new attitudes have been expressed organizationally by the Zero Population Growth movement.

In order to achieve zero growth, women, on the average,

would have to limit themselves to 2.1 children each, a process
that would halt population growth in seventy years if begun
now. This, it will be observed, is not far below the indicated
current level; and many demographers believe that the U.S. is
already on the road to zero growth.

The ZPG organization was launched in September 1969, prin-
cipally by Paul Ehrlich, the Stanford biologist; it had 8,000
members by April 1970, and has about 35,000 members now.
But the real significance of the ZPG idea goes beyond these
numbers. It lies in the larger fact that the *concept* of a nongrow-
ing population has taken root in the thinking and vocabulary of
large numbers of educated people, and has even achieved recognition by government (e.g., there is now an official Census Bureau projection based on zero growth). Automatic approval of
large families has quietly gone out of style.

Any set of policies designed to curb population growth needs
to take immigration into account. Immigration has recently run
around 400,000 annually. It is coming increasingly from the
Americas and Asia; and Europe, which once accounted for 80
percent of immigrants, now provides only about one-third. Net
immigration has been contributing 20 percent of total population growth — and perhaps 70 percent of the net inflow to metropolitan areas. And since most immigrants are on the youngish
side, the nation's population totals will eventually be increased
further by the immigrants' children and grandchildren.

But some of the new uncertainties may be impinging on the
net immigration figures. More and more Americans are leaving
the country permanently. A recent study by Richard Irwin of the
Census Bureau states: "There is evidence that emigration has
increased considerably since 1965. This may well be a temporary
phenomenon, but at the present time emigration may be 30,000
per year or more, and is increasing." The increase seems to reflect some of the new concerns about U.S. society; those leaving
it are apparently seeking to go where life is less crowded or the
frontier more open than in the U.S., or to escape social disorders,
crime, or a deteriorating environment.

Another force for slowing population growth may be govern-

We May Be On the Way to ZPG

Total births are well below the levels of a decade ago, but they started to increase in 1969 and seem bound to continue to do so until at least 1980, if only because so ma young women will be arriving at the main ages of childbearing. All three of the Cen Bureau projections charted here seem within reach; a fourth, which assumed that women on the average would have 3.1 children each in the 1970's, already seems beyond reach.

The "C" projection assumes that they will try for 2.8 children each. The "D" projec tion assumes an average of nearly 2.5, which is actually about the current pace of ch bearing. The projection labeled "ZPG" refers to an average of 2.1 children, a rate at which population growth would eventually slow down to zero. Some demographe think we are already approaching that rate.

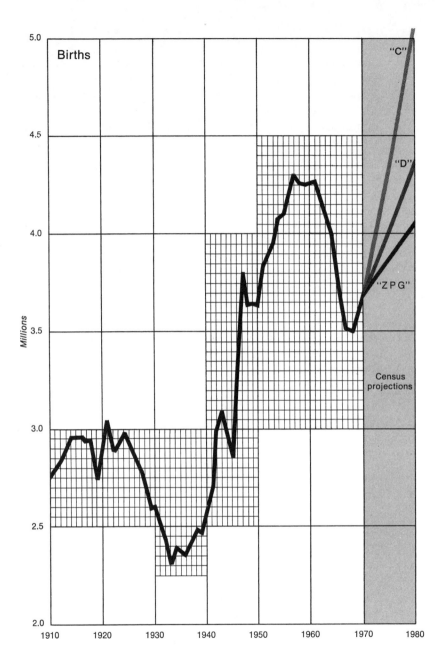

ment policy. The Ninety-first Congress authorized the first major federal expenditure for birth control. It would allow the government to spend $235 million over the next three years to establish and expand family-planning services operated by local authorities as well as by nonprofit hospitals and organizations. An additional $145 million has been authorized, much of it to finance research to discover better and cheaper methods of birth control. States are making abortion legally available far more widely than before; substantial liberalization, legislative or judicial, has already occurred in eighteen states and the District of Columbia. And part of the rationale of all the various attempts to upgrade the poor is to bring down their above-average birth rate. Both sign and symbol of all the underlying currents is President Nixon's creation of a Commission on Population Growth and the American Future. In authorizing it, Congress specifically provided that "The Commission shall conduct an inquiry into . . . the various means appropriate to the ethical values and principles of this society by which our Nation can achieve a population level properly suited for its environmental . . . and other needs."

Distributing the people

The Administration's main concern about population just now is not to slow its growth — that has been happening anyway — but to do something about its distribution in the U.S. "Population location is policy-responsive," says Daniel P. Moynihan, who is a former counselor to the President and is concerned about distribution. It is true that the government has all along influenced the location of population in various ways — through FHA-guaranteed mortgages to home buyers in the suburbs, highway construction, defense contracts, etc. — but in all such cases the location was only a side effect of some other policy. Now there is real interest in some conscious direction of population flow. Without it, the belief in Washington and among social scientists and geographers runs, the U.S. is heading for a future in which most of its people will live in a dozen or so huge metropolitan complexes, each consisting of several large cities joined together by enormously extended suburbs. Left behind will be, loosely speaking, an immense barren hinterland.

Population, of course, has been spilling out of the farms and Main Streets of the Midwest for decades. In the 1960's the principal losses were suffered along a belt running southward from North Dakota, as well as from the Mississippi Delta eastward through West Virginia and into southern Georgia. The main destinations of this migration were the Far West, the Northeast and down the Atlantic coast as far as Virginia, as well as Florida and some areas around the Great Lakes. About two-thirds of the more than 3,000 counties in the U.S. actually had more out-migrants than in-migrants in the past decade. But because many of the losers also had sufficient natural increase of population, only half of all U.S. counties wound up the decade with fewer inhabitants than they had in 1960.

The historic movement into metropolitan areas continued during the 1960's. As a result of natural increase plus migration, 75 percent of the nation's population growth occurred in the Standard Metropolitan Statistical Areas (which are defined as counties in which a central city of at least 50,000 people is located, plus adjacent counties economically and socially linked with the city). However, the population increase of the metropolitan areas was smaller, both absolutely and relatively, than it had been in the 1950's. Their smaller relative growth casts at least some doubt on that widely accepted notion that almost all Americans will be living in huge, sprawling urban areas by the year 2000. There is, in fact, some evidence from the new census suggesting that population growth is occurring just beyond the present metropolitan areas.

Bigger gains in smaller places

Furthermore, it is the medium-sized rather than the largest metropolitan areas that have been growing the fastest. Of the top

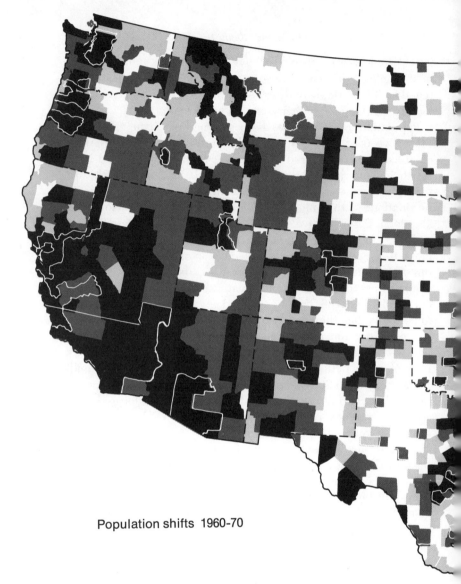

Population shifts 1960-70

Who's Moving Where

During the last decade, people left many of the middle areas of the U.S. and tended to move toward the coasts; about 53 percent of the population now resides in states on the coasts (including the Great Lakes). Some such "move from the middle" has been going on for about forty years. However, in the 1950-60 decade, more of the losses were concentrated along a horizontal line across the corn belt rather than along the North-South axis of the past decade. There has been increasing interest in de-

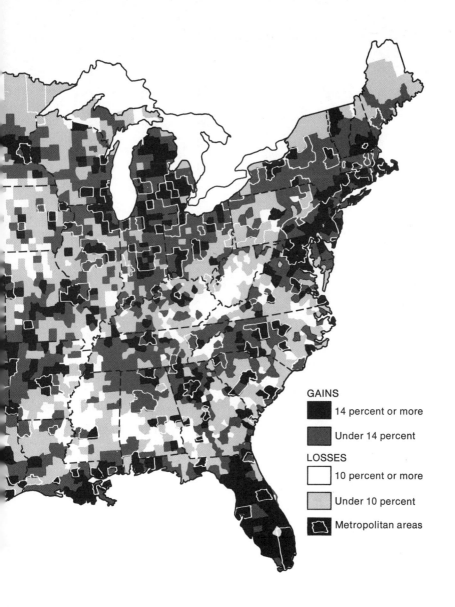

GAINS

■ 14 percent or more

▨ Under 14 percent

LOSSES

□ 10 percent or more

▨ Under 10 percent

⬡ Metropolitan areas

oping a government policy to influence the distribution of population and minimize
owding.
e map does not delineate all of the more than 200 metropolitan areas in the U.S.,
Fortune has not separated those that adjoin one another (note the large blocs on
California coast). This blending emphasizes the extent to which Americans now
e in adjoining urban regions increasingly identified by the term "megalopolis."

U.S. population 1970

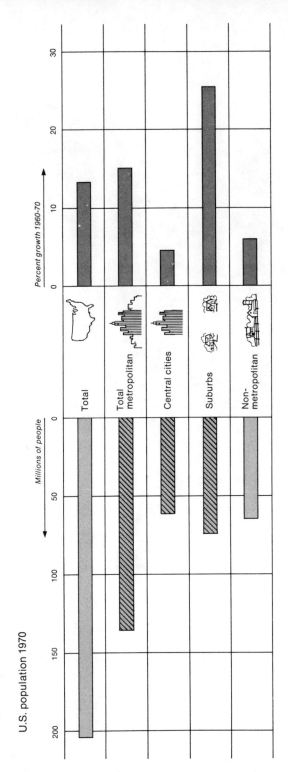

Millions of people

Percent growth 1960-70

Total	
Total metropolitan	
Central cities	
Suburbs	
Non-metropolitan	

Who's Moving Where

In the chart above, the bars on the left side show that 136 million, or about two-thirds, of the 205 million people in the U.S. in 1970 resided in metropolitan areas. The chart also points up the continuing shift to the suburbs; more people now live in them than in central cities. Suburbs grew about 25 percent in the past decade (bars at right); the central cities and all nonmetropolitan areas taken together also gained, but at less than half the 13.7 percent pace of the entire nation.

twelve, all with more than two million people, only Los Angeles, San Francisco, and Washington, D.C., grew more rapidly than the national average, and the Washington area was the only one to grow appreciably faster. But twenty-three of the thirty-one metropolitan areas that now hold 750,000 to two million people increased more than the national average: these big gainers were Houston, Minneapolis–St. Paul, Dallas, the Anaheim, California, area, Seattle, Atlanta, the Paterson, New Jersey, area, San Diego, Miami, Denver, the San Bernardino area, Indianapolis, San Jose, New Orleans, Tampa–St. Petersburg, Portland, Phoenix, Columbus, Rochester, San Antonio, Dayton, Sacramento, and Fort Worth.

It is scarcely surprising that most of the growth in metropolitan areas continues to be in the suburbs. In the 1950's the suburban rings grew four times as fast as the central cities; in the 1960's they grew five times as fast. Thus the population densities of the urban areas are still declining, as they have been since 1920. Sixteen of the twenty-five largest cities in 1960 had lost population by 1970: Chicago, Philadelphia, Detroit, Baltimore, Cleveland, Washington, St. Louis, Milwaukee, San Francisco, Boston, New Orleans, Pittsburgh, Seattle, Buffalo, Cincinnati, Minneapolis (New York City gained slightly even though Manhattan's population fell 11 percent and Brooklyn's 2 percent).

There are substantial disagreements about whether and how population distribution patterns might be changed. Many students of urban affairs feel that any center with fewer than 250,000 people may not be able to provide enough services and economies of scale to be attractive to business and therefore to be self-nourishing. Some evidence is turning up, however, that much smaller areas can be nudged toward more growth. Analysts in Washington have been compiling lists of urbanized areas consisting of 25,000 to 50,000 people, which have been gaining population. The analysts believe that these might well be the nuclei of new growth centers. And Calvin Beale, a demographer in the Department of Agriculture, claims that, contrary to the conventional wisdom, less densely populated areas have actually not done badly in recent years. His data show that, when you

SNAPSHOTS OF A CHANGING SOCIETY

Much of the swirling change that left so many Americans feeling their world was ofte[n] unrecognizable in the 1960's was the product of the dramatic demographic changes reflected in these charts — some of which also project substantial change for the 1970's. The charts below and at right show that the most significant increases in the past decade were among people in their teens and twenties, who were prime instiga[tors] of change. In this decade, however, many of the same people will be in their thirties and more inclined to settle down. Tremendous gains in educational attainment are still taking place (chart on page 46), and by 1980 about half of all young people — and 40 percent of young blacks — are expected to have attended at least one year of college.

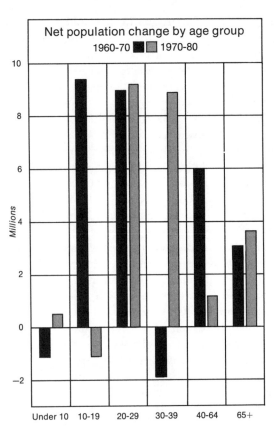

Net population change by age group
1960-70 ■ □ 1970-80

Millions

Under 10   10-19   20-29   30-39   40-64   65+

Growing Up in the 1970's

There will be fewer teen-agers [by] 1980, but about nine million m[ore] Americans in their twenties and another nine million in their thirties. Comparatively few peo[p]le were in their thirties — the peak home-buying ages — in t[he] past decade.

here has been a sharp decline in poverty according to official figures (chart on page 7); but some argue that the figures, which are only adjusted for cost-of-living increases, should also reflect Americans' continually rising living *standards*.

he last chart reflects the Bureau of Labor Statistics' projection of changes in occupa-onal structure from 1970 to 1980, assuming G.N.P. growth of about 4.3 percent a ear. Should full-employment growth be substantially less, demand for skilled white-ollar and service workers is likely to increase less than projected; much higher growth an 4.3 percent, conversely, may create more high-skill jobs than projected.

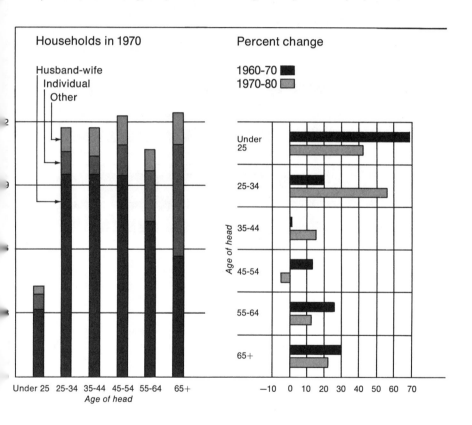

Households on the Rise

The number of U.S. households increased by about one million a year in 1960-70; in this decade they should increase by 1,300,000 a year; although the case may get to seem less clear-cut if new communal and other living arrangements begin to change notions of what a "household" is.

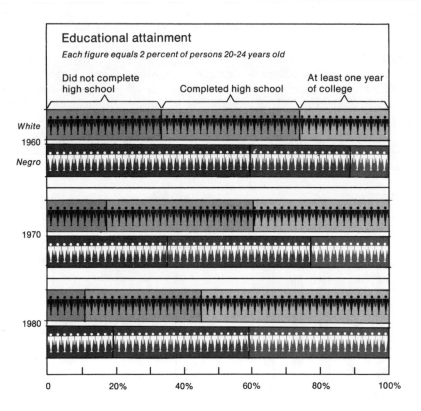

Educational attainment

Each figure equals 2 percent of persons 20-24 years old

Did not complete high school | Completed high school | At least one year of college

White 1960

Negro

1970

1980

0   20%   40%   60%   80%   100%

The Widening Road to College

Despite increased misgivings about mass higher education, the 1970's are still apt to see a continuing massive move to college by both whites and blacks. Overall educational attainment among young Negroes in 1970 was about equal to that of whites in 1960; in 1980 it should almost equal the white record of 1970.

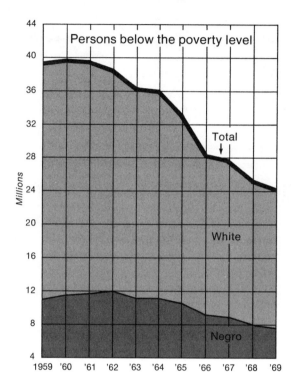

Persons below the poverty level

Total ↓

White

Negro

Millions

1959 '60 '61 '62 '63 '64 '65 '66 '67 '68 '69

The Official Line on Poverty

On the Social Security Administration's "official" definition, a
family of four with an income of less than $3,721 was living in
poverty in 1969. (In 1959, when living costs were lower, the
cutoff was $2,943.) The number of people in poverty dropped
by almost 40 percent, to 24 million, from 1959 to 1969. The
decline for whites was about 25 percent more rapid than for
Negroes.

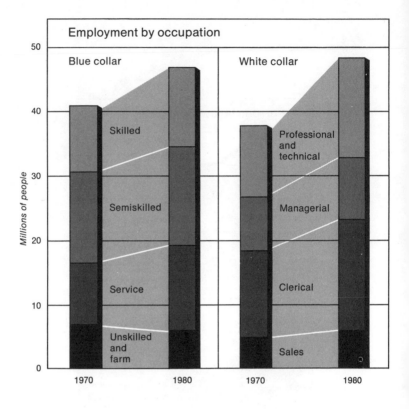

White-collar workers will continue to increase rapidly in the 1970's, and by 1980 there will be more white than blue collars, even when service workers are considered to be "blues." Among white collars, the managerial group will grow least because it includes retail proprietors, whose ranks are not increasing.

exclude farm families, the population of nonmetropolitan areas has been growing *more rapidly* than the national average, and employment in these areas is up markedly. He ascribes a good deal of this job growth to the fact that the labor-force participation of women in rural households, long far lower than for women elsewhere, is rising rapidly.

There are some disagreements, not only about where to distribute population, but about how to do it. For example, should programs concentrate on helping population centers that are beginning to flourish, or on trying to rescue those in decline, or on building new towns? There is also dispute as to whether the government should put its emphasis on direct financial assistance or on coordinating its indirect influences on local growth — e.g., through all those decisions affecting highways, defense installations, and university centers.

New options for women

One new uncertainty about all future U.S. population totals — and about quite a few other matters — concerns the somewhat altered relationship between men and women. Some sociologists believe that the alterations will be extended dramatically by the effects of the women's liberation movement. Philip Hauser of the University of Chicago remarked recently that "the role of woman is changing from that of female to that of human being"; he believes that the change implies an entire new range of options for women, and that as a consequence they may be less inclined than in the past to view marriage and a family as their main concerns in life.

Indeed, statistics on marriage during the 1960's suggest that young women are already somewhat less disposed to rush into it than formerly. Between the prewar years and the late 1950's, the median age of first marriage declined by 1.8 years for men and 1.3 years for women. But in the past dozen years the median age of first marriage has turned back up by about a half year or so (in 1970 it was 23.2 for men, 20.8 for women). Because they are marrying later, the rate of marriage among young people has declined.

It is interesting to note, however, that the total number of marriages has *not* declined. The highest of a set of Census Bureau marriage projections made in 1967 has actually been exceeded — and this projection assumed that marriages would take place at the high rates of the past. How can the over-all rate stay at a high level when young people are deferring marriage? One possible explanation runs as follows: Divorces have been rising — in 1970, for example, they went up approximately 12 percent, to some 740,000. Thus the marriage totals may be getting a lift from *re*-marriages, which may be up enough to compensate for the lag in first marriages.

But what explains the continuing lag in first marriages? It won't do to blame the Vietnam war. After the 750,000 or so extra men went into the armed services during the 1965–66 buildup, the number in service stabilized as discharges offset inductions. Nor does it seem probable that more widespread adoption of the pill and of contraception generally have reduced marriages precipitated by pregnancy: the evidence available suggests that there are as many pregnant brides as ever (somewhat more than 20 percent of all brides).

Part of the explanation for the lag in first marriages has to do with new mores. Couples today live together in premarital trial runs more freely and in greater numbers than ever before. "These days," observes one Census Bureau demographer, "you don't have to be married to have a mate." You certainly don't have to be married to have company, as the varied new communal living arrangements among young adults make clear. The spread of such practices may be holding down the number of first marriages temporarily; trial runs may even be persuading some people that they aren't suited for marriage.

Settling down at twenty-five

Thus far the new arrangements seem to contribute to delaying — rather than replacing — marriage. Census data show a noticeable shortfall in the number of husband-wife households whose heads are under twenty-five, as the marriage data suggest. But the number of married couples in which the husband's age is between twenty-five and thirty-four is about 9,550,000, quite close to the Census Bureau projection. Apparently, just about all the young people who could have been expected to settle down finally did so.

The data at hand on marriage and families contain hints of changes in American life styles, and in the so-called life cycle. A middle-class family's cycle has typically involved early marriage, three or four children, a house in the suburbs and two cars, commuting, the wife working part time when the children are in their teens, trying to squeeze in some travel and savings and perhaps college for the children, and then coming to terms with — or feeling relieved about — a childless home.

Now consider the emerging variation on this theme. The couple marry later and the wife works longer before the first child. She is apt to have only two children and to go back to work while they're still quite young — all of which tends to improve the family's financial situation considerably. Largely because wives as well as husbands expect to be employed most of the time, couples may increasingly want to live in homes near their jobs. All along they will have wide options — e.g., whether to save more, to increase their stocks of consumer durables and clothing, or to spend freely on recreation and travel.

Fred Davis, a University of California sociologist, suggests that some of the new mores are apt to affect spending habits. He believes that many young couples are already displaying less interest in buying bedroom sets or houses. Many of them are simply not concerned about the same kinds of creature comforts that were sought after by previous generations. Explains Davis: "After several years of hitch-hiking around the country with a sack on their backs and sleeping on the floor in countless crash pads, those kids who do decide to rejoin straight society have a far different view of what they want out of life than did other groups."

The new mores are making it more difficult to interpret the census data on households. A young man and woman who are not married but are living together may not admit the relationship to the census interviewer and therefore may end up being counted as one or perhaps even as two individual households. It is also hard to know how some of the living arrangements that have developed in many large cities and college communities show up in the bureau's statistics. Instead of several airline stewardesses, say, or several young executives, sharing an apartment, some young men and women are jointly occupying entire houses or large apartments in groups of as many as thirty.

THE RISING TIDE OF WOMEN WORKERS

Proportion in the labor force

	1950	1960	1970
All women	31.4%	34.8%	42.6%
All married women, husband present	23.8	30.5	40.8
With children under 6 years	11.9	18.6	30.3
With children 6-17 years only	28.3	39.0	49.2
With no children under 18 years	30.3	34.7	42.2

One piece of evidence of the changing role of American women is the increasing proportion who work; even those with small children have moved heavily into the labor force. About two-fifths of all married women are in the labor force and 70 percent of all employed women work full time, although less than half of them work year-round.

Some of these communal living habits result from the housing shortage and attempts to hold down expenses. In other communes, whether the participants are single or married, the purposes are to explore new ways of living and of sharing experiences in accordance with the precepts of economic, social, religious, philosophical, or sexual theories — sometimes of several theories at once. A survey by the New York *Times*, published in December 1970, uncovered 2,000 urban and rural communes of all types, and this may be an undercount of 1,000. A typical commune had between five and fifteen persons. A group in Marin County, California, where the *Times* reported several dozen hippie-style communes, is planning a city of 20,000 for those who wish to live communally.

J. L. Aitken, a psychologist at Dow Chemical, believes that the communes, particularly those in universities, are building a new version of the family. At some future time, he expects, groups with tight-knit interpersonal relationships will not only share their food and shelter but will want to work as a group and will command the skills to be hired as a group. Indeed, there is one communal group teaching at the School of Art and Architecture at Yale.

Teen-agers in decline

One reasonable certainty about 1980 concerns the age structure of the population then: everyone who will be over nine years of age at that time has already been born. As the chart on page 44 indicates, some significant changes in the age structure of the U.S. population are in store, and they imply some large social changes. In the 1960's there was a tremendous increase among teen-agers and people in their early twenties; the number of ten- to twenty-four-year-olds grew by 15,500,000 in ten years. This increase made all kinds of "youth markets" suddenly important in the decade. It also led to higher unemployment totals (the rates among teen-agers tend to be higher than those for mature workers). In the same period there was a decrease — a sort of "population hollow" — among people thirty to thirty-nine, a fact that helped many executives in their twenties climb the career ladder rather quickly.

In the decade ahead, the teen-age markets will wane, for the number of ten- to nineteen-year-olds will actually decline a bit. There will be another large increase of people in their twenties, but this time their career opportunities will be more limited because large numbers of people in their thirties will, in a sense, be standing in their way. This roadblock may be partly relieved by continued rapid gains for those in their thirties, who are still trailing that population hollow.

The merger of jobs and education

The rapid increase of people in their twenties, many of whom have new values, life styles, and attitudes toward work, will create a number of new uncertainties about the U.S. labor force. For example, Harvard sociologist Lee Rainwater surmises that many of today's well-traveled young people may want to decide in which part of the country they want to live and get a job there — rather than take a job wherever it is offered. Further, many young people want at least part of their careers to be devoted to the alleviation of social problems; young lawyers, doctors, and business-school graduates are already devoting a fair amount of time to improving the conditions of ghetto residents. Other young people refuse to make permanent career commitments at all; they teach for a couple of years, for example, then go off to something like leather crafts for a while. In fact, there is a suspicion around — although admittedly no comprehensive statistics back it up — that students are not committing themselves to college the way they once did; many more appear to be dropping out, spending some time working or drifting, then perhaps going back to school. The University of Chicago's Philip Hauser believes this process may finally come to seem normal — i.e., we will get used to large numbers of students, even doctoral candidates, alternating between school and work.

Edwin Harwood, a sociologist at Rice University, has noted that lower-status teen-agers — especially the boys — also differ from their predecessors. He points out that nowadays even a young man who is poor is apt to have lax work disciplines because in a wealthier and more humane society he is relieved of "a compelling need to make a serious commitment to the labor force. He does not support the family."

Another emerging large question about the labor force concerns the match-up between education and jobs. Some who have studied the relationship believe that many job specifications ask for more education than is actually required. As a result, some otherwise qualified applicants are rejected, overqualified workers develop unrealistic expectations or frustrations about their prospects, and the nation's educational resources are misallocated. The chart on page 46 shows the tremendous gains in educational attainment of the past decade. It projects a slower increase to 1980 because educational levels — especially for whites — are already so high. About 40 percent of white youths now attend college for at least a year, and at least 17 percent graduate.

There is certainly nothing new about the fact that the economy and its demographics are changing. In earlier years those changes generally involved an intensification of past trends or moves toward the evolution of a more sophisticated and richly endowed society. But now all the familiar old assumptions about the desirability of "bigger and better" possessions have come under fire, and the question of what really is "better" is in dispute, whether the subject is the standard of material wealth or the best style of family life. It is apt to be quite a few years before a new consensus is arrived at.

Three

"Identity Crisis"
in the Consumer Markets

Americans are increasingly trying to "express themselves"
— to help fashion their own identities — in what they buy.
Some are expressing themselves in a sweeping decision
against material goods.

One of the characteristics of the age we live in," Walter Lippmann wrote in 1929, in *A Preface to Morals*, "is that we are forever trying to explain it. We feel that if we understood it better we should know better how to live in it, and should cease to be aliens who do not know the landmarks of a strange country."

What was true then is even truer now — and for businessmen and economists, no less than for sociologists, moralists, literary critics, and sundry other intellectuals. When a group of corporate executives were asked in December 1970 to list books they would like to give and to receive as Christmas presents, they named Charles A. Reich's *The Greening of America* and Alvin Toffler's *Future Shock* more often than any others. However much one might fault the businessmen's critical judgment, their selections indicated a deep malaise about, and an unassuaged hunger to understand, what has been happening to American life and culture.

Their hunger is understandable. Cultural, social, and political forces impinge on the economy more directly now than they have in a long time. As a result, there is more uncertainty about the long-term outlook of the economy than during most of the postwar period.

The largest uncertainty involves the direction of American life and culture. Are Americans embracing a set of values so different from those of the past that they add up to a whole new outlook on life and work and society, as Yale's Professor Reich, the leading guru of the new Consciousness III, argues? Are the alienated young "giving shape to . . . the saving vision our endangered civilization requires," as Reich's fellow prophet, Theodore Roszak, argues in *The Making of a Counter Culture?* Or has the dream of a new drug-centered hedonism turned into a nightmare, as John Lennon, one of the authentic heroes of the counterculture, now argues? (In a January 1971 issue of *Rolling Stone*, Lennon proclaimed that "the dream is over," and added: "I'm talking about the generation thing. It's over, and we gotta — I have to personally — get down to so-called reality.") Do the extraordinary popularity of *Love Story* and the apparent decline of political activism and revival of traditional collegiate activities mean that the bulk of the young are still squarely in the mainstream of American life and culture? Or does the truth lie somewhere in between?

The questions go to the heart of the outlook for the various markets for consumer goods and services. If Reich, Roszak, Marshall McLuhan, and similar prophets are even remotely close to the mark, the consumer market would be totally transformed by the end of this decade. There would be major shifts in the pattern of expenditures; more important, with large numbers of Americans gripped by an antimaterialist ethic, there would be a drastic reduction in the attractiveness of consumption itself. Any such lower propensity to consume, together with a parallel reduction in the incentive to work hard, or even to work at all, would mean lower over-all levels of income, hence of spending, and a slower rate of growth of productivity, and thereby of the economy's productive capacity.

The new era of fads

What are the probabilities of such a shift occurring over the next decade or so? The answer is complex, if only because of the diversity of American life. A large majority are still devoted to work and consumption, but a new hedonism and an antimaterialist rhetoric (not always translated into actual life style) do seem to be taking hold among a small and influential minority. It is too soon, therefore, to make any firm judgment about how these divergent tendencies will balance out — all the more so because, in recent years, Americans have been buffeted by frequent shifts in tastes, with apparent trends in one direction being replaced with incredible rapidity by trends in the other. Thus George N. Shuster of Notre Dame speaks of "the tyranny of the transitory," and Professor Zbigniew Brzezinski of Columbia University refers to the present as "the age of volatile belief" — an "era of fads, of rapidly shifting beliefs, with emotions providing some of the unifying cement previously supplied by institutions and with the faded revolutionary slogans of the past providing the needed inspiration for facing an altogether different future."

The volatility is the result of the merger of two deep-seated trends of long duration. One is the widening of individual choice that the diffusion of affluence has provided; the other is an erosion of faith and tradition stemming from the growth of rational, skeptical, scientific modes of thought. The era of fads is apt to last a long time. Fads are furthered by the mass media, which have replaced tradition as the arbiter of taste and style. As a result, the new styles adopted by the avant-garde are quickly diffused to the rest of society — which makes the members of the avant-garde search restlessly for still newer styles.

Homogenizing the workers

The enlargement of individual choice has been in the making for a century and a half or more, but it has accelerated greatly since the end of World War II. When most families earned barely enough to pay for food, clothing, and shelter, they had little scope to exercise choice. And this was the condition of the great majority of Americans before the postwar era. In 1929, which used to be considered a pretty good year, 70 percent of all family units earned less than $5,000, in dollars of 1970 purchasing power, compared to 30 percent today; only 15 percent earned $7,500 a year or better, compared to 56 percent today. Understandably, therefore, the consumer market was divided between a small "class" market and a huge and relatively undifferentiated mass market, in which the great bulk of expenditures went for necessities.

The postwar boom, with its steady growth and diffusion of affluence, transformed and "homogenized" the consumer market. The tendencies toward homogenization were the result of the many demanding and gaining the amenities of middle-class life, amenities that a few decades earlier had been limited to the few. With more and more discretionary income at their disposal, waiters and chefs, plumbers and carpenters, machinists and auto and steel workers, could choose to drive the same kinds of cars, wear the same kinds of clothes, and take the same kinds of vacations as did clerks, salesmen, teachers, businessmen, and professionals.

Increasingly, individuals' decisions as consumers got to be bound up with their notions of the life styles they wanted. And as more and more workers chose to live in suburbs or in the outer reaches of large cities, away from the old working-class neighborhoods, the blue-collar style came closer to that of the white-collar middle class in other ways as well. The most striking change, perhaps, was the shift in workers' orientation away from the all-male clubbiness and sociability of the local bar, poolroom, firehouse, or club, and toward their homes and family life. This, in turn, reduced the traditional sharp distinctions between blue-collar and white-collar mores with respect to husband-wife relationships. This was dramatically evident in blue-collar husbands' new-found willingness to help with the supermarket shopping, or with the dishes — as well as in child-rearing practices and the pattern of recreation and socialization.

Most want to work

This process of *embourgeoisement*, as some sociologists call it, is still going on, and is likely to continue throughout the 1970's.

The appeal of an antimaterialist ethic seems in general limited to the well-to-do; it is scarcely conceivable that the 60 percent of Americans — some 40 million family units — with incomes of less than $10,000 a year today will gravitate away from materialism. Certainly, the 20 million family units with incomes of less than $5,000 would like nothing quite so much as to "make it" into the middle class and its traditional values. An equal number of family units, moreover, find their energies bound up in the struggle to get more of — or merely to hold on to — the middle-class amenities they have only recently attained. Indeed, most of the ten million family units earning between $5,000 and $7,500 a year and many of the ten million in the $7,500-to-$10,000 bracket would be surprised to learn that they have much discretionary income at their disposal. In the last few years, certainly, their incomes have been devoured by the spiraling costs of food, housing, medical care, and, for a growing number, a college education for their children.

Far from being sated with goods, most Americans would like to consume more, and are willing to work hard in order to do so. And younger household heads appear to be more, not less, consumption-minded than their elders; 73 percent of household heads under thirty-five years of age surveyed by the University of Michigan's Survey Research Center said they had unsatisfied wishes, compared to only 36 percent of those fifty-five years or older.

One result of this intense desire for more is that income has become discretionary in a radically new sense: increasingly, the *size* of a family's income — and not just the way it is allocated — is a matter of discretion. Instead of spending being a function of income, as John Maynard Keynes argued, income is becoming a function of spending, or, more precisely, of the consumption pattern or life style that people want to achieve or maintain. In order to live and consume in the desired manner, families may elect to raise their income: wives go to work; husbands moonlight or work overtime; and either may enroll in courses or training programs that enable them to move up the income ladder.

The process works both ways, of course, and some Americans are plainly opting *against* higher incomes and more consumption. Many of the alienated young — for example, the nonstudents who congregate around the fringes of large universities (the current favorites are Harvard, Berkeley, and the University of Kansas), the young men and women who can be seen hawking plastic flowers, jewelry, or underground newspapers on street corners of cities like New York and San Francisco — move in and out of the labor force with some frequency, taking a job only when they are flat broke and quitting when they have a little money. Others work more regularly — e.g., at making leather sandals, or weaving, or at other low-paying handicraft jobs that don't offend their antimaterialist sensibilities.

The great majority of younger Americans, however, are seeking all the leverage they can to increase their incomes. More than half the married men in the twenty-five- to forty-four-year-old group, for example, have working wives. Some 40 percent of the men work overtime, and nearly one in ten moonlights; of all household heads holding second jobs, in fact, half are under thirty-five. And there would appear to be a lot of untapped desire to work more. Among household heads approached by the Survey Research Center, for example, 49 percent of those under thirty-five expressed a preference for more work, and only 7 percent for less.

A majority of Americans, then, are continuing to make the kind of life-style decisions that reshaped so many consumer markets in the 1960's. The question faced by these Americans has been, ultimately, a fairly simple one. It comes down to whether or not to identify with the still-growing, predominantly suburban, casually materialist middle class. In the 1970's, it appears, a substantial minority of Americans who are already in the middle class will have some more complex decisions to make.

First, there is the fundamental decision about whether to opt for work, income, and consumption — i.e., whether even to stay in the middle (or upper) class. For those who do elect to stay, there are further decisions. For that homogeneous-looking middle class of the early 1960's has been increasingly fragmented in recent years. More and more of its members find a need to differentiate themselves from others — to express, in both their career decisions and their spending habits, something of their own individuality. The consumer markets of the 1970's, it seems clear, will be profoundly affected by an increasing insistence by the customers on using consumption to express themselves, to help in the fashioning of their own identities.

Durable trends in spending

These new forces in the marketplace are hard to find in the broad statistics of consumer spending and saving, which show no break with the patterns of the postwar period. During the 1960's consumer spending kept pace with the growth in G.N.P. and personal income; an 87 percent rise in disposable (i.e., after-tax) personal income between 1959 and 1969 produced an 86 percent growth in consumer spending, from $311.2 billion to $577.5 billion. As was the case in the late 1940's and 1950's, moreover, and as one would expect from economic theory, consumers increased their spending on durable goods a good bit faster than they did on nondurables. The former increased by 103 percent (from $44.3 billion in 1959 to $90 billion in 1969), while spending on nondurables went up 68 percent (from $146.6 billion to $245.8 billion). In the same period, spending on services rose 101 percent (from $120.3 billion to $241.6 billion). Since the prices of cars, appliances, home furnishings, and other consumer durables increased less rapidly than the price of nondurables and services, the disparity was even greater in physical terms. Measured in dollars of constant purchasing power, that is to say, consumers increased their purchases of durables by 94 percent against a 37 percent increase in purchases of nondurables and a 55 percent rise in outlays for services.

There were no real discontinuities, moreover, in the way consumers allocated their incomes among the various categories of durable and nondurable goods and services. Thus the proportion going for food has continued to decline as income has risen, in accordance with one of the oldest laws of economics. The proportion of expenditures allocated to purchases of clothing, transportation (including new cars), and household operation hardly changed during the 1960's, while the proportion going for medical care, private education, personal business (insurance premiums, brokerage charges, and the like), recreation, and foreign travel has continued to increase at a modest rate.

But this over-all stability in the basic patterns of consumer spending masks a good deal of change and even turbulence within individual markets. The most interesting markets these days are several in which the new demands for self-expression are becoming major themes. Not surprisingly, the clothing market has become something of a bellwether.

Excitement in men's underwear

It was only a decade and a half ago that "the man in the gray flannel suit" was the symbol of uniformity in dress and thought. If an individualist has any complaint today, however, it is that in the explosion of color, shape, style, and so on, anyone who happens to *like* gray flannel suits may have a hard time finding one. Increasingly, males are expressing their individuality in a "peacock revolution." What used to be considered purely functional items are increasingly subject to fashion and style; as a television commercial asks, "Who says that men's underwear has to be dull?" At the same time, however, men are also asserting their right to comfort — hence the collapse of the market for suits and the boom in blue jeans, slacks, and other comfortable leisure clothes.

For increasing numbers of Americans, the clothes they wear are not simply material objects; on the contrary, they are viewed, sometimes with almost mystical fervor, as the most basic expression of life style, indeed of identity itself. This, of course, is why

the alienated young and their middle-aged mentors and advocates cling with such fervor to blue jeans, bell bottoms, and long
hair; their style of dress symbolizes both their rejection of middle-class culture and their assertion of their own counterculture.
(The same fact, of course, explains the passionate anger and
venom with which the "hippie style" is viewed by so many
parents of the alienated young and other members of the
parents' generation.)

One consequence of this demand for self-expression is that department stores have had to experiment with new ways of ar-
ranging their merchandise. Federated Department Stores, the
largest U.S. department-store chain, is searching "for a better
definition of its markets — one that will lead to a sort of resegre-
gation of the merchandise," according to Barry Miller, the
chain's director of consumer research. Instead of segregating
women's clothing by type (dresses, coats, suits, etc.), and then,
within each type, by age and price (junior, misses, women's,
"better dresses," etc.), Federated outlets now typically devote all
or most of a floor to clothing that expresses particular "states of
mind." One floor might be for mod fashions, for example, another for conservative fashions. Thus many large stores are
turning into groups of boutiques.

The boutique phenomenon is evident in furniture and other
home goods and accessories, which are used these days to express states of mind too. Home-goods stores are increasingly specialized — there are even some that specialize in the new water-
filled mattresses. Furniture stores are becoming smaller and they
tend to specialize in a particular style, e.g., modern, colonial.

This specialization, like the self-expression it is abetting, has
been accompanied by a growing variety of materials, fabrics,
colors, and styles. Not too long ago, the only choices consumers
exercised in buying what are called white goods — sheets, pil-
lowcases, etc. — had to do with quality and price. Today the
term itself involves a kind of cultural lag, for sheets and pillow-
cases that are actually white now account for only 40 percent of
the market. Manufacturers of these products began to offer vari-

ety in the 1950's, when customers first had a choice of fitted (contour) or plain sheets, each available in several solid colors; now the choice extends to a wide array of prints, stripes, patterns, and solid colors.

Self-expression at home

The need felt by many Americans to express themselves cannot work to expand all the consumer markets of course, and it may work to hold down some — especially those markets in which it is difficult to project one's own highly individualized life style. Some parts of the housing market may be confronting such difficulties today. Single-family homes have lost heavily in competition with apartments and mobile homes. Some shift to apartments had been expected, of course, as a result of demographic changes; apartments are often preferred by young couples without children or with only one, and more and more couples are both deferring children and having fewer these days. In recent years, however, apartments have accounted for far more new construction — they were 41 percent of all units built in 1970, up from 15 percent in 1959 — than can be explained in purely demographic terms. Even the special difficulties in financing single-family homes during the financial squeeze of 1969–70 do not seem to explain all that "extra" demand for apartments. Anthony Frank, chairman of the San Francisco Federal Home Loan Bank, speculated recently that young consumers may simply prefer to spend their money on other amenities — and minimize their commitments to housing.

The consumers' search for self-expression has had a somewhat different effect on the $35-billion auto market. As in the furniture market, but in contrast to men's clothing, there is a pronounced shift in consumer taste from the flamboyant (lots of chrome and large fins) toward what one industry economist calls "simplicity, austerity, and utility." While talk of austerity may be somewhat exaggerated — most Americans, after all, insist on automatic transmission and power steering, and a growing number equip their cars with air conditioning, stereo tape players, power windows, and other sybaritic extras — the market *has* shifted toward smaller cars with cleaner lines. The shift does not seem to reflect a desire to save money for other amenities, but, rather, a positive preference for smaller cars. Market researcher Daniel Yankelovich speaks of a tendency for people to "wear their car" rather than merely to own it — to see it as an extension of their personality rather than as a manifestation of their status. Thus owners of Volkswagens and other foreign cars see themselves as more sensible and down to earth than the mass of Americans; owners of sports cars and the imitation sport types see themselves as youthful swingers, and so on.

There is less correlation, therefore, between the price of a car and its purchaser's income — particularly because of the steady increase in the number of two (and three and four) car families. At least one family in four now owns two or more cars, compared to only 10 percent in 1955; these families usually choose different kinds of cars, reflecting the different personalities of husband and wife and different life styles of parents and children.

In many ways, the markets most profoundly affected by the new tendencies toward self-expression are those involving leisure. In the past, one of the most striking differences between Americans and Europeans was that the former tended to define themselves by their vocation, the latter by their avocation. Herman Kahn, the wide-ranging savant who heads the Hudson Institute, has observed: "When you ask a European what he does, instead of saying he's a clerk, he is likely to say, 'I'm a motor driver,' or 'I'm a mountain climber.'" Americans are tending in this direction; what a man does with his leisure is perceived, increasingly, as a key to his identity. Boating enthusiasts — nearly nine million Americans own boats — identify themselves as a breed apart from golfers, and neither resembles bowlers or Sunday painters; among boating men, moreover, the sailing fans see themselves as distinct from (and superior to) the outboard-motor crowd.

A split in the markets

Self-expression is not the only factor affecting consumer spending, of course; in many consumer markets an insistent demand for convenience is also a major theme. Convenience is apt to be associated with simple mass-produced goods, whereas self-expression generally implies many varieties and options. In many markets, then, a major split is now visible.

Take, for example, the rapidly growing markets for cameras and hi-fi equipment. Camera bugs these days can opt for a quite individualized approach to photography. They can buy a seemingly endless variety of cameras, lenses, filters, flash attachments, lights, developing and enlarging equipment, and other complicated paraphernalia that will enable them to produce photographs that are very much their own. Alternatively, they may opt for convenience, in which case they have an almost equally large choice of easy-to-operate, indeed almost foolproof, equipment. Much the same is true with hi-fi equipment. The consumer may elect to assemble, from a vast array of sophisticated components, an intensely individual stereo system that suits his own ear. Or he can choose any of a number of prepackaged compact systems.

Some such split is also discernible in the $132-billion market for food and beverages. The big growth has been on the "convenience" side of the line. Per capita consumption of processed (canned and frozen) vegetables increased during the 1960's, while per capita consumption of fresh vegetables declined. Consumption of frozen and packaged pies and cakes, "brown and serve" rolls, and cake and cookie mixes has been soaring, at the expense of home-baked products. Higher purchases of frozen fish sticks, portions, and fillets have increased per capita consumption of fish (contrary to the general expectation that consumption would drop when the Catholic Church lifted its ban on eating meat on Friday).

Consumers' willlingness to pay for convenience in their food is of course an outgrowth of affluence, which has made time as well as money a scarce resource to be allocated among competing uses. It is only as discretionary income rises that people begin to see time as a resource to be optimized. When convenience foods were first introduced early in the postwar period, Americans were still uncomfortable with the notion of leisure, and manufacturers found that they had to de-emphasize the saving in time and energy in order to assuage women's feelings of guilt. In the 1970's the guilt feelings are pretty much gone. "Treat yourself to a one-hour vacation," the makers of Swanson's frozen TV dinners urge housewives in a television commercial — which shows a mother using the "vacation" to finger-paint with her daughter.

But the growing use of convenience foods is paralleled by a burgeoning interest in gourmet cooking. When preparing the family's meals ceases to be an overwhelming daily chore, women — and men, for that matter — can begin to see cooking as a form of recreation and self-expression. Hence the popularity of relatively sophisticated televised courses like Julia Child's on gourmet cooking, and the seemingly limitless market for gourmet cookbooks (a market whose size undoubtedly has been enlarged by the new interest in ethnic differences). This democratization of *haute cuisine* is paralleled by a boom in consumption of table wines. Those whose taste buds have been elevated but who prefer to spend their time outside the kitchen can choose from a rapidly growing variety of frozen and canned gourmet foods.

The new engine of change

Given the manifest vitality of most consumer markets, and the continuing eagerness of most Americans to spend money, why should there be any uncertainty at all about the durability of the traditional belief in work and consumption? None of the changes in consumer behavior we have been describing, after all, involve any real break with the patterns of the past. The new emphasis on self-expression, for example, is simply a logical extension of a change whose beginnings *Fortune* noted in 1959 — which involved an increasing tendency of consumers to choose, not merely this or that item of merchandise, but this or that style of life.

The main reason for viewing the traditional values as vulnerable is the U.S. economy's extraordinary success in creating abundance and widening choice. In the process, the economy tends to undermine the very values that made the success possible. This process has actually been at work since the 1920's, when, as sociologist Daniel Bell suggests, the high-consumption economy made possible by mass production began to undermine the values associated with the Protestant ethic, replacing them with a new and hedonistic materialism. The essence of the Protestant ethic was an emphasis on prudence in consumption, delayed gratification, and work as its own reward. "But the claim of the American economic system," as Bell points out, "was that it had introduced abundance, and the nature of abundance is to encourage prodigality rather than prudence. The 'higher standard of living,' not work as an end in itself," thus became the engine of change, and "the glorification of plenty, rather than the bending to niggardly nature," became the justification of the system.

For a long time the change was obscured by the fact that Americans still paid verbal tribute to the old virtues of the Protestant ethic and seemed uneasy about abandoning them. As recently as the 1950's it was often pointed out that Americans did not know how to play and, indeed, tended to dread free time. Corporate managers provided the most striking manifestation of how uncomfortable most Americans felt about having fun; typically, senior executives justified their vacations as a means of increasing their productivity on the job. ("I'm going away to recharge my batteries.") Many still feel this way; but a growing number of Americans are beginning to see work not as an end but as a means — in particular, as a means of earning enough to enjoy themselves, and express themselves, when they are *not* working.

Understandably, new attitudes are most visible among the

younger, more highly educated, and more affluent members of society, who are most insistently seeking a new balance between work and leisure. A recent survey of attitudes among Americans of high-school and college age taken by Louis Harris & Associates for *Life* indicates that while the young are not about to renounce money as one ingredient in the search for personal fulfillment, they clearly are looking for less rigorous paths to fulfillment than previous generations followed. Asked how they would use their leisure if their regular job took care of the family's needs, for example, 88 percent of the young people said they would "relax and enjoy life with family and friends" and 85 percent indicated that they would "pursue a hobby, sport, or recreation"; only 26 percent said they would get a second job to add to their income.

This is not to suggest that the hedonistic attitudes of the counterculture are certain to prevail. There is in fact some evidence suggesting that the counterculture is losing some of its glamour, and that the young may be rediscovering at least some of the middle-class virtues. The psychiatrist Erik Erikson of Harvard, who is perhaps America's leading student of adolescence and youth, has suggested forcibly that the new behavior patterns of the young in the 1960's may not represent any wave of the future at all. Erikson believes that "the available inventory" of pleasure-seeking experience will be tried by the young and found only moderately satisfying, and "new boundaries will then emerge from new ways of finding out what really counts." Their judgment about what it is that "really counts" is perhaps the largest of all the uncertainties about the U.S. economy in the years ahead.

Four

Autos:
A Hazardous Stretch Ahead

Some of the romance is out of America's affair with the automobile. Detroit nevertheless expects plenty of growth in the 1970's.

Public discussion of the auto industry these days is so heavily centered on the large uncertainties created for it by new environmental and safety regulations that it will doubtless come as a surprise to learn that there is still a "standard forecast" in Detroit. What's more, the forecast is pretty optimistic about the coming decade. The consensus shows a trend line of unit sales increases averaging 3.5 percent a year — a rate that yields a "normal" annual volume of 11,300,000 cars by 1975 and 13,200,000 by 1980. Right now the record for U.S. sales is the 1968 total of 9,600,000 cars (1970's total was 8,400,000).

And so the first point to note about Detroit's standard forecast is that it anticipates market growth of some 40 percent during the decade. The second point to note is that in Detroit the forecast is viewed as moderate. There are some optimists around who look for gains of more than 50 percent.

There is no doubt that the standard forecast has a lot going for it. There will soon be well over eighty million cars on the road, each with a useful life span averaging about ten years; they will provide a basic annual demand approaching eight million, simply to replace those that wear out. Demand should also rise with population. General Motors' forecast is based on a population of 228 million by 1980. And gains will be largest in the twenty-five to thirty-four age bracket, whose young households have historically represented most of the growth in auto ownership. Virtually all of this growth will be concentrated in the suburbs, where, on G.M.'s projection, 47 percent of all Americans are expected to live by 1980. The forecast also assumes that disposable personal income will almost double, to $1.343 billion, by the end of the decade. Suburban living combined with rising income has historically meant increased multiple car ownership: Some Detroit economists expect the proportion of families with two or more cars to increase from the present 30 percent to 37 percent.

All of this may sound as though the auto industry's economists have never heard of the new imponderables in the market — and in the U.S. economy — but that is not the case. Henry Duncombe, the low-keyed director of economic studies at G.M., knows very well that there is a catch about all such projections nowadays. So do Duncombe's counterparts at the other auto companies. "We may be sitting on a bomb here," admits Kenneth C. Merrill, assistant controller of Ford Motor Co. They note that their time-honored formulas may now be overmatched by an array of elements that nobody has learned to quantify or even to anticipate accurately. And so another point has to be made about the standard forecast: it is ventured with less confidence than it used to be.

The first three chapters have pointed out the sources of the new uncertainties. Fundamental questions are being raised about the economic, demographic, and sociological trends underpinning all business. There are unprecedented new questions about the number and size of families; about how many persons will choose to work and how hard they may be willing to work; about their propensity to take the fruits of increased productivity in the form of increased leisure rather than consumption; and about the manner in which they will spend their disposable income. There are also questions about the extent to which Americans will embrace an emerging antimaterialist ethic that is implacably hostile to any form of conspicuous consumption.

It gets from here to there

The auto industry, producing the most expensive item (apart from a house) that most Americans ever buy, has a special interest in the answers to such questions. In addition, it faces some problems peculiar to itself. The most fundamental is the fact that the attitude of many drivers toward their automobiles has changed in important ways. In a recent book, *Aspirations and Affluence,* Dr. George Katona of the University of Michigan's Survey Research Center and two co-authors observe that studies conducted in the late 1960's "indicate that the car has increasingly become a means for serving important ends, rather than the highly prized possession it once was in the United States and still is in much of Europe." Many people — especially better-educated, higher-income young adults — now view their cars in a more rational, more matter-of-fact, and less emotional way. They see the cars as equipment that gets them, more or less comfortably, from here to there; they are less susceptible to the industry's traditional sales pitch, which has often been directed at status-conscious households and has encouraged them to trade up to the limit of their ability. Hence the sales of Cadillacs, Lincolns, and Imperials have not risen as rapidly as the number of households whose incomes once would have marked them as prime prospects. This is not to say that a majority of the buying public has become determinedly utilitarian. But practicality has replaced glamour as the primary consideration of an important segment of the market.

This tendency is closely related to the rising demand for second and third cars, which have in fact represented virtually all the industry's sales growth in recent years: since 1960, the number of cars owned by one-car families has risen by only 1,800,-000, while multiple car households have added more than nine million to the auto population. "Because of differences in the purposes for which the cars were to be used," Katona and his co-authors remarked, "frequently two different types of cars were wanted." In that case, "even prestige obviously did not require that the second car be large."

The most visible consequences of the second-car boom have been a proliferation of models and an increase in smaller cars; both trends may be said to have culminated in the recent introduction of American cars to compete directly with vehicles of Volkswagen size. Over 56 percent of the new cars delivered in 1970 were imported or domestic small cars, compact models, and

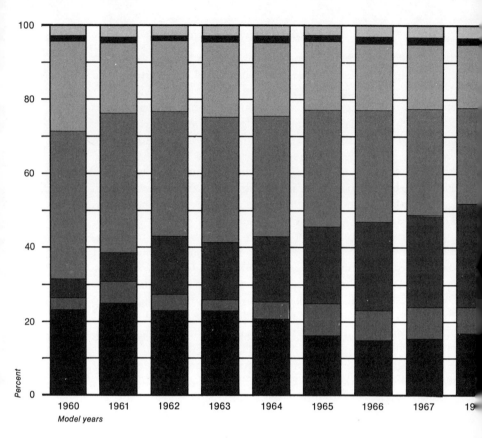

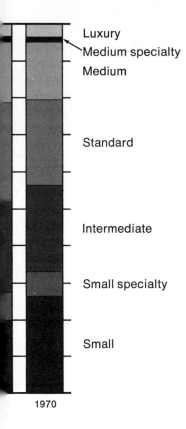

Luxury
Medium specialty
Medium

Standard

Intermediate

Small specialty

Small

1970

The Spending Patterns Are Changing in the Auto Market

The full-size Chevrolet, Ford, or Plymouth used to be the standard American car, but the market share taken by such models declined steadily during the 1960's. Early in the decade they came under heavy competitive pressure from small cars (i.e., foreign and domestic models of compact size or less), whose own sales then fell off sharply in the middle 1960's as U.S. manufacturers' compacts grew to intermediate size (Chevelle, Torino). The small cars were also hit hard by the popularity of the small specialty makes like the Mustang and Camaro. But these cars in turn have started to fade badly and, although the intermediates are now holding their own, models in the lowest size and price bracket are staging a dramatic resurgence. The comeback of the small car, bolstered by a steady rise in demand for second and third cars, is expected to continue throughout the decade. For the first time, Detroit is battling the foreign invaders head to head with subcompact economy lines of its own: G.M.'s Vega, Ford's Pinto, American Motor's Gremlin, and Chrysler's two captive imports — the Japanese-built Colt and the English-built Cricket. Meanwhile, the markets for luxury cars and the medium specialty models (Toronado, Thunderbird) have scarcely grown.

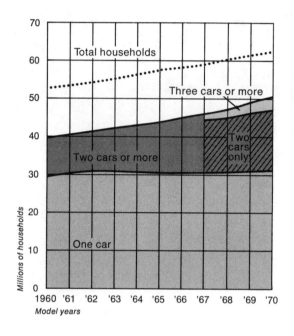

Millions of households

70
60 Total households
50 Three cars or more
40
30 Two cars or more | Two cars only
20
10 One car
0

1960 '61 '62 '63 '64 '65 '66 '67 '68 '69 '70
Model years

Demand for second and third cars has been the main source of the auto industry's growth in recent years. The number of one-car households has barely risen, from 29,800,000 to 31,600,000 over the decade, and the number of carless families has declined slightly. Multiple car ownership has followed a trend line almost precisely paralleling the growth in total households since 1960.

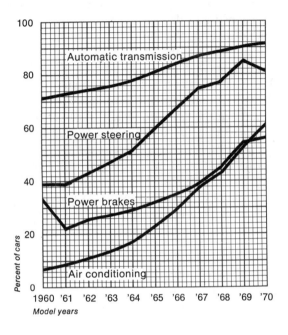

Percent of cars

100

Automatic transmission

80

60

Power steering

40

Power brakes

20

Air conditioning

0

1960 '61 '62 '63 '64 '65 '66 '67 '68 '69 '70

Model years

Despite the trend to smaller automobiles, sales of cars equipped with extra-cost optional equipment have continued to climb sharply to high levels. The success of air conditioning, the most expensive option offered on most cars, has been especially impressive. Sales of power steering, however, have turned down along with the popularity of big cars, and orders for power brakes appear to be leveling off below the 60 percent range.

so-called intermediate vehicles like the Chevelle and Torino. Ten years ago the intermediate and smaller cars had less than 32 percent of the market. And the trend is expected to continue. Henry Ford II looks for the compacts and subcompacts alone to capture 35 percent of 1971 sales.

More ominous, from the industry's point of view, are signs that Americans, having almost stopped loving their cars, may begin to hate them. The car's association with pollution has already led to what might be called an anti-auto ideology among some of the young, and to such bizarre ceremonies as that ritual burying of a car at the San José State College campus in February 1970. At least there is no doubt that Detroit has to live with criticism on an entirely new scale. Donald E. Petersen, vice president of car planning and research for Ford's product-development group, admits, "More and more people view the automobile as an unfortunate necessity. As you are viewed more as a necessity, people are less tolerant of your shortcomings."

The view at the leading edge

Katona and his collaborators suggested much the same thing. Their interviews, they wrote, "revealed that the major problems confronting consumers no longer concerned the car purchase itself." Instead, attention is now focused on problems that arise after the purchase: quality of construction, resale value, parking, congestion, insurance, and repairs. John Riccardo, president of Chrysler, predicts that "whatever type of car the customer buys, he is going to be more and more concerned about how well it works and whether he can get it serviced and repaired."

The correspondence files of the Federal Trade Commission, the President's Office of Consumer Affairs, the Senate Commerce Committee, and a variety of private consumer agencies are bulging with thousands of letters from drivers detailing such problems with their vehicles. The companies acknowledge that there is rising customer dissatisfaction, and some detect worrisome signs that it could grow worse in the future. Petersen of Ford is remarkably candid about the distressing results of a recently completed study of people that he describes as on "the leading edge of opinion" — younger, better educated than the norm, with higher-status jobs and above-average incomes. "There was a significant negative attitude — a pro-foreign, anti-Detroit syndrome," he says. "Mercedes was the ultimate, although these people might never have had one. People believed that we make too many changes for change's sake — nonfunctional changes. There was a credibility gap. People don't believe our advertising. It has almost done more harm than good."

The clearest visible reflection of such attitudes was the dramatic leap in sales of imported cars in the period before President Nixon's New Economic Policy. (Admittedly, the NEP changed the prospects of all importers quite a bit.) In 1970, while sales of American-built models tumbled 15 percent from the year before, imports gained 12 percent to a total of 1,250,-000. One car in seven sold in the U.S. is built overseas. Typically, they are bought by the same avant-garde group surveyed in the Ford study, but the acceptability of owning a foreign car is clearly spreading throughout the population. Moreover, thanks to their reputation for quality and to their improving service, the foreign manufacturers have begun to penetrate the higher-profit fields beyond the subcompacts. In 1970 Volvo sales rose to nearly 45,000, Mercedes-Benz sales rose to 25,000, and the newly introduced German Audi sold 7,700 units in its first seven months on the market.

Now that the invaders have established such a firm beachhead, there is a question whether they can be repelled even by the truly small cars that the American companies have just brought out: G.M.'s Vega, Ford's Pinto, American Motors' Gremlin, and Chrysler's Japanese-built Colt and English-built Cricket. G.M. predicts that sales of imports in 1971 will be off only about 100,000 from 1970 in spite of the tougher competition. And one of its U.S. competitors actually envisions a slight further rise in imports. Stuart Perkins, president of Volkswagen of America, is confident that the attention focused on small cars by Detroit advertising will actually help his firm's sales prospects. "People are looking at small cars who weren't looking before," he explains, "and they look at us." His dealers still have waiting lists, he says, and "in the last quarter [of 1970] we could have sold 50,000 more without effort. Every shipload is sold." The enormous success of VW, which sold over half a million cars in the U.S. in 1970, has been greatest among the young.

American manufacturers can take comfort in the fact that even antimaterialist youth, enamored of a new life style, still want the mobility cars provide them. The manufacturers' problem is that when you begin to regard cars as *nothing more* than a key to mobility you may end up gravitating naturally to the homely German Beetle rather than a high-powered Detroit product.

The cost of regulation

There is no doubt that the nation's new concerns about pollution and safety have fortified the more critical attitudes toward cars; and also no doubt that the critical attitudes have made it easier for government to adopt a tough stance toward the auto industry in dealing with the concerns. Ford's studies, Petersen says, demonstrate that "people are ready for more legislation. We should assume this and be aware of it." Thus the carmakers' most immediate problem is government intervention in the design of automobiles. Among the most crucial questions arising from this unparalleled new intervention: How much will new requirements add to costs? Can these costs be offset sufficiently to avoid large price increases? If not, how will buyers respond? And what will changes in demand mean to the companies' profitability?

Of all the new requirements, the most attention thus far has been focused on the exhaust-emission-control devices required by Senator Muskie's amendments of December 1970 to the Clean Air Act. Under its terms, carbon monoxide and hydrocarbons must be reduced 90 percent from 1970-model levels by the 1975 model year (unless the government grants a one-year extension). A year later, emissions of nitrogen oxides must be lowered 90 percent from 1971-model levels. Auto-company executives are rather evasive about what the antipollution equipment may cost. Publicly, they declare that they have no reliable figures; their private estimates range all the way from $100 a car to $300.

The latter figure is probably high. Some government officials scoff at this latter figure as wildly unrealistic, and designed merely to frighten politicians wary of enraging their car-buying constituents. Certainly the record of the industry's economy-conscious engineers suggests that they will somehow find a way to minimize the initial cost of the antipollution devices. Assuming, that is, that they can produce the devices at all in time for the 1975 model year. Lee A. Iacocca, Ford's president, is one who doubts that they can. "We will never make the Muskie deadline, in my opinion," he declares flatly. But the industry itself is divided on the question, and Ford's chief Washington agent now believes the standards will be met. Vice President Rodney W. Markley Jr. argued forcefully, in his lobbying against the bill, that the standards could not be met by any technology in sight. He lost badly — in the Senate by a 73-to-0 vote. Now he predicts, "Detroit will make a liar out of me, and I'm glad."

Wanted: a new engine

There are those who think it would be better to find a substitute for the internal-combustion engine. The Administration has already given the industry a nudge in this direction. Early in 1970 President Nixon's ad hoc panel on unconventional vehicle propulsion concluded that the carmakers were not making a substantial effort to develop alternatives to the internal-combustion engine. The panel report was followed by a two-part program involving government-sponsored independent research and incentives to private manufacturers to develop alternatives. Through fiscal 1975, $73 million is scheduled to go into the federal research effort; sixteen R. and D. contracts have already been signed. Another $20 million will go into the incentive programs, under which the government will purchase and test prototypes turned out by private manufacturers. Cars that establish the best rating on low emissions will be frankly favored in the government's fleet purchases of some 20,000 vehicles a year.

At least four possible alternatives to the present standard engine have already received significant attention:

• The German Wankel rotary engine, which General Motors is developing under a nonexclusive contract that costs the company $10 million a year, may be the best bet in the near future. Although it is also an internal-combustion engine, it is radically different from the conventional reciprocating types. Right now the Wankel engine produces even more hydrocarbons than these; but its pollution problems can be eliminated with relatively cheap exhaust afterburners, and the engine's small size and light weight make it easier to fit the devices under the hood. Considerably more development work must be done, however, before the system can begin to look like a real threat to the reciprocating engine.

• The gas-turbine engine, which Chrysler installed in experimental automobiles years ago, is still probably about a decade away from acceptable performance standards. And it, too, poses emission problems — in this case, too much nitrogen oxide.

• Battery-powered electric cars, about which Ford scientists were excited in the late 1960's, are now regarded as very long shots. Even if they are produced they will almost surely have severely limited range and usefulness. By increasing the demand on the nation's electricity-producing plants, moreover, electric cars could actually *add* to the total volume of pollutants poured into the atmosphere.

• The steam engine has the most vocal backers of any of the proposed alternatives. A 1969 report of the Senate Commerce Committee staff, "The Search for a Low-Emission Vehicle," gave it a glowing endorsement and called it "a satisfactory alternative to the present internal-combustion engine in terms of performance and a far superior engine in terms of emissions."

Car manufacturers are skeptical of all these alternatives and, inevitably, more comfortable working with a power plant that they have developed and manufactured over many decades. If they can clean up the internal-combustion engine in time to meet the Clean Air Act's standards — and most of them appear to believe that they can — they see no reason for a crash program to replace the engine. They are hedging their bets with cautious research programs, but right now none sees a serious possibility that the current engine will be displaced in the Seventies.

A fast-moving target

Unless they are compelled to abandon their present engine, the companies enjoy at least one advantage in dealing with the emissions problem. They have a fixed target: the requirements of the Clean Air Act are stringent, but there is at least little likelihood that they will be increased. The case is quite different with respect to safety, where at least thirty-four new standards have been proposed in the last four years.

There is no doubt that the new standards will add to the price of cars. One conspicuous example is the demand for a "passive-restraint" system to replace seat belts — which are effective when used but require the rider's active cooperation and more often than not go unused. The National Highway Traffic Safety Administration has ordered all manufacturers to install, by mid-1973, passive-restraint equipment to protect a car's front-seat occupants from serious injury in a head-on collision at thirty miles an hour. So far, public discussion of such equipment has centered on air bags, which are designed to inflate automatically and instantaneously in a crash to keep driver and passengers from being tossed around in the car's interior. Although the companies are not compelled to use air bags as their passive restraint, Administrator Douglas W. Toms has warned that he will seek eventually to increase the speed at which passive restraint is effective; and at those higher speeds, he contends, only something like the air bag will meet the requirements. The companies have complained that they cannot overcome a variety of engineering difficulties by the 1973 deadline and are looking at stop-gap measures. They also doubt that buyers will willingly pay the higher prices associated with the bags. Chrysler recently proposed to substitute a system of energy-absorbing cushions on the dashboard, and others hint that they may follow the same course. The cost of the Chrysler equipment, estimated by company engineers to be only half that of air bags, would still be $50 to $75 per car.

In recent months, the N.H.T.S.A. has begun stretching its original mandate — the protection of human lives — to cover reduction of damage to the vehicle itself. As the industry is uneasily aware, changes designed to protect the vehicle might also get to be expensive.

The first step in this direction was the recent order that auto manufacturers standardize the height of their bumpers and improve their shock-absorbing capacity. At present, the bumpers on many cars do not meet those on many others in collisions, and so protection on all the vehicles involved is reduced. Moreover, even when today's bumpers meet a stationary obstacle directly, they will protect a car from serious damage only at speeds below three miles an hour — which is why simple parking-lot collisions frequently produce repair bills running into hundreds of dollars. The new standards, supposed to apply to 1973 models, would raise the level of protection only to five miles per hour. Senator Philip Hart, the Michigan Democrat, asserts that this modest improvement will save at least $1 billion a year in damage. The companies say they may not be able to meet the deadline, and some intend to install shock-absorbing bumpers on the front only. Even that, they predict, will add $50 to the cost of each car.

Making them easier to fix

There is also strong support in Washington for government standards on auto-damage resistance and repairability. The appeal of reduced repair costs is not hard to see. An official of the American Mutual Insurance Alliance recently reported that the average auto-damage claim has risen by 111 percent since 1960. The Insurance Institute for Highway Safety estimates that a 1970 Chevrolet Impala, striking a concrete test barrier at just fifteen miles an hour, would sustain $740 worth of damage. Insurance-industry officials are expected to back a bill sponsored by Senator Hart that would require the Department of Transportation to establish standard test procedures for damageability and then to publish comparative results for cars by make and model.

The impact of all the new rules on costs is obviously conjectural at this point. But the possibilities are alarming to many auto executives. Roy D. Chapin Jr., chairman of American Motors Corp., has warned that regulations already in sight could add $600 to the cost of an average car. What's more, since most of the antipollution and safety equipment has a relatively fixed cost, it will have the greatest effect proportionally on the price of the smaller, more economical models to which the customers increasingly have been turning. It's true that the foreign imports will also have to meet the standards, but Ford's Iacocca points out that "in Japan they will do it for $1.50 an hour, and we will be paying more than $7."

The extent to which the new costs can be passed on is also conjectural. Improved damage resistance and repairability have a demonstrable value and will ultimately save the car owner money on both repairs and insurance premiums; in time they could pay for themselves. On the other hand, that higher price associated with the new standards will have to be paid before the buyer ever realizes any savings. Moreover, it will be years before the new standards are incorporated into a majority of the cars on the road, and so insurance companies may be slow to reduce rates.

Since the manufacturers will have trouble merchandising the new design standards and equipment as greater value, and since the changes will plainly entail higher prices, Detroit is now looking hard for areas where money can be squeezed out of their vehicles. The most obvious place to cut substantially is in the vast expenditures that now go for annual and biennial styling changes. These might be reduced in two ways — by stretching out the frequency of major model changes and by making the changes themselves less striking. The chances are that both will be done. Executives at all of the companies say that the two-year major-change cycle is a thing of the past. The manufacturers have also announced that they will keep their new small cars unchanged in style for as long as five years.

There are real risks in any such strategy, which represents a reversal of the industry's traditional way of doing business. If styling and "newness" are as important as the companies have always assumed, less frequent and modest changes may cut heavily into basic demand. Some executives argue that the proliferation of models — the creation of many different models with specialized functions — will help solve the problem and ensure plenty of variety in the showrooms.

A $3,000 Pinto in 1975?

But even a concerted effort to hold down costs may not succeed. Iacocca has suggested that the new regulations, combined with a 5 percent rate of inflation, could make the Pinto, which now sells for less than $2,000, a $3,000 car by 1975. That is surely an extreme — and unlikely — possibility. But 10 or 15 percent increases are anything but improbable. And nobody is at all certain of the impact on the market of any such substantial price boosts.

Surprisingly, none of the companies has done a satisfactory study on the price elasticity of demand. They say that so many factors affect car demand (e.g., disposable income, consumer confidence, credit availability and cost, as well as the appeal of new styling) that it is almost impossible to single out the influence of higher prices. Until recently, moreover, automobile prices had been remarkably stable. The Bureau of Labor Statistics' year-end index for 1970 put car prices at only 111.9 percent of the 1957–59 level; the comparable index for all consumer prices was 138.5. The University of Michigan's Survey Research Center's studies indicate that average net expenditures per car (after trade-in allowance) rose only 23 percent between 1958 and 1968.

Consumers might respond in a variety of ways to higher prices. Very few are likely to give up automobiles altogether. (The proportion of households without a car continued to decline in the 1960's, and is now only about 20 percent.) The nation's transportation system is built around the private passenger car. Martin Wohl, director of transportation studies for the Urban Institute, says that the traffic pattern of every metropolitan area — not just Los Angeles — is so random that no public system could compete effectively with the private car for most riders. Traffic does not converge on the most centralized city, he points out. "Half of the cars going through the Lincoln Tunnel into New York at the morning rush hour simply cross Manhattan and go somewhere else."

But if Americans will continue to insist on having cars, price increases may well prompt them to drive their vehicles a bit longer than they otherwise would. And this could work to reduce sharply the scrappage rates that, in effect, form the solid base of auto demand. It is true that scrappage rates are being pushed up in some ways: the soaring cost of repairs and the increased difficulty and expense of insuring deteriorating autos have contributed to higher rates. However, these are areas in which federal regulators are showing more interest, and their actions might work to hold scrappage down in the future. And rising used-car prices, which encourage owners to feel that the models they're driving are worth repairing, could further tip the balance in favor of keeping older cars running longer.

The most probable consequence of major price increases will be reinforcement of the already evident trend, rooted to a large extent in Americans' new values, toward purchase of smaller, more economical cars. This will have a severe impact on dollar sales and on profitability. Manufacturers' percentage-profit margins are higher on higher-priced cars; the dollar profit on a vehicle at the top of the line can be five or six times that on the lowest-priced model. A general downgrading all along the line would have a substantial cumulative effect on profits.

What's more, smaller cars mean fewer extra-cost options — and the margins on many options are far greater than those on even the most expensive basic vehicle. About two-thirds of Ford's Mavericks, for example, are equipped with automatic transmission, while nearly 99 percent of the full-sized Fords have it. And only half of Chevy II Nova buyers take power steering, compared with 90 percent of big Chevrolet purchasers.

The uncertainties facing the auto industry, then, are formidable. So, it must be said, are the industry's determination and confidence. Nobody is underestimating the difficulty of satisfying government officials, keeping prices down, fighting off the challenge of foreign autos, and fanning the flames of the legendary American romance with the motorcar. But almost nobody in Detroit shows any signs of pessimism. Executives there believe firmly that for this decade, at least, the car will remain king.

Five

Famine Years
for the Arms Makers

It will take a major wrench in public attitudes about defense
to end the industry's private depression.

When some household detergents were recently banned on eastern Long Island, Llewellyn J. Evans, the effervescent president of Grumman Corp., was moved to discharge a terse comment on the future of defense and space contracting. "It's no different from detergents," he said. Not that Evans himself has reason for inordinate gloom. Grumman's sales and earnings are holding up relatively well, and its employment is down "only" 25 percent in the past two years. Moreover, it has been awarded the contract for the Navy's new F-14, the world's most sophisticated combat plane; Grumman's total revenues on the project may well add up to more than $10 *billion* by the time production ends.

Nevertheless, as a comment on the state and general prospects of the U.S. space and defense industry, Evans' remark was much to the point. The exhilarating business of fabricating advanced weaponry and space vehicles, long used to operating profitably in the outer reaches of high technology, has come to earth with a thud. Cutbacks in military and space spending have left the industry mired in its own private depression and apprehensive about its future.

Defense contractors have always known that their industry involved massive uncertainties. Even if military business were expanding at a fairly uniform rate, it would be neither steady nor predictable for individual operators. Just getting into it is an uncertain process; North American Rockwell spent $25 million in bidding on the F-15, the Air Force's new fixed-wing combat plane, only to lose the job to McDonnell Douglas. Much of the industry's output consists of novel, uneconomic, fantastically complex and expensive weapons whose most crucial problems are simply unforeseeable. So space and military contracting, far more than even civilian capital goods, is the archetype of feast-or-famine operations.

Such are the uncertainties facing the industry today that it can hardly look forward to expanding at all, much less to expanding at a uniform rate during the Seventies. Among the most important of these uncertainties is one rooted in a whole new range of antiwar attitudes, including some that are highly rational and some that are largely emotional. The source of these new attitudes is not entirely clear, but something more than the unpopularity of the Vietnam war seems to be involved. It may be that mass higher education has created a numerous new intelligentsia, devoted to humanist causes and intolerant of policies that entail human suffering, whose attitudes have doomed old-fashioned patriotism. Whatever its source, the new pacifism is powerfully affecting the willingness of large numbers of Americans to support a huge defense establishment.

A second uncertainty arises out of massive new disagreements about the kind of establishment that is needed in the 1970's — i.e., about the nature of the threat we will be facing. A strong case can be made today that the Soviet Union is more powerful in relation to the U.S., and more menacing to American interests, than it has ever been in the past. But it is also possible to argue that the cold war is, or could be, just about over — or even that warfare in general soon will become obsolete.

Finally, there are new uncertainties about the esoteric method of arriving at a military budget. The process is being re-examined for the excellent reason that no one — including the manufacturers, the Administration, Congress, and antimilitarist intellectuals — is satisfied with it. The criteria for deciding whether we need various defense "goods" remain unclear, and the terms on which the goods are supplied too often involve either windfall profits or catastrophic losses. Reorganization of the entire process is necessary; and reorganization itself might critically affect the size of the defense market.

These uncertainties, in one way or another, have already left their mark on space and defense contracting. Total military spending has not declined very much from its 1968 figure of $78 billion — at least not when the total is measured in current dollars. But procurement, i.e., of weapon systems, research and development, construction, and sundry supplies and services, has taken the rap. In fiscal 1972 procurement will have dropped to $36.4 billion from $45.4 billion in fiscal 1968; in constant 1971 dollars, the decline is 31 percent, from $51 billion to $35.3 billion. On top of that, space outlays by NASA will have dropped from about $4 billion in 1968 to $2.5 billion. (And on top of *that*, the civilian aircraft business, upon which most big defense contractors depend heavily, is also in the dumps.) Thus the space and military market, which a few years ago seemed destined to go on expanding indefinitely, has suddenly shrunk from nearly $60 billion to less than $40 billion in 1971 prices, a decline of about a third.

"An unbelievable dissipation of talent"

The shrinkage has had large social consequences, extending far beyond the health of the defense industry itself. Everywhere in the industry regiments of skilled people have been tossed out on their ears. The heavy layoffs reflect two peculiarities of the space and weapon business: it uses inordinate numbers of man-hours per unit of output, and its normal employment per unit of output tends to fluctuate widely, rising steeply as a product goes into production and falling steeply as production increases and the "learning curve" improves. The combination of contract cutbacks and rising learning curves has thrown about a million and a half workers in the industry out of jobs.

The workers involved were among the elite members of the U.S. labor force. As the repository of a disproportionate amount of the nation's high technology, the defense and space industry employs an unprecedentedly huge proportion of engineers and scientists — in aerospace one for about $150,000 of sales, compared to one for every $750,000 of sales in consumer electronics like television and one for perhaps every $2 million in the auto

The rising cost of capability

One reason it is hard to keep military spending down is that weapon systems are growing steadily more capable, complex, and costly. Take the fighter plane. For about eleven years the F-4, or Phantom, in a round dozen variations, has been the standard U.S. fighter. McDonnell Douglas has sold more than 3,750 to the U.S. military as well as more than 250 to other countries. Recent delivered price: around $3 million per plane. But to keep up with Soviet competition, the Navy some time ago began to plan on the F-14, a supersonic swing-wing fighter. After entertaining five bids, it awarded the engineering-development contract to Grumman. Just how much an F-14 will ultimately cost is not entirely clear; in any case, Grumman has recently indicated that it will have trouble meeting the original bid price. The official estimate in March 1971 was still $11,500,000, but few would be surprised if the total moved several million higher.

What will the F-14 have that the F-4 doesn't have? It will be considerably faster than the F-4, which has done 1,600 mph. Owing to its expensive swing-wing construction, which at subsonic speeds gives it a 64-foot wingspan (against 38 for the fixed-wing F-4), it has much greater lift. In combat it can accelerate 40 percent faster and climb twice as fast as the F-4, and turn in a 40 percent smaller radius. Not only can it stay in the air twice as long, but it has twice the payload or weapon capacity: i.e., it can carry the same payload twice as far or twice the payload the same distance. Its weapons include an M-61 gun as well as six Phoenix, four Sparrow, and a number of Sidewinder missiles. Its radar will have more than twice the range of the F-4 radar, and its missile range is four times as great.

The F-14 will weigh little more, fully loaded, than the F-4. The engines, which will develop 40 percent more thrust, will actually be lighter than the F-4's. Weight was saved everywhere. Titanium in the structure between the two wings saved about 1,100 pounds (as compared with steel). And such materials as boron epoxy in horizontal-tail skin surfaces, fiber-glass epoxy on the nose, and acrylics for windshield and canopy also saved hundreds of pounds.

industry. The number of engineers and scientists at work in the industry — the totals include some in commercial aerospace — has declined from 223,000 in 1968 to 154,000. "This represents an unbelievable dissipation of technical talent," laments Donn Williams, vice president of North American Rockwell. "And it is getting lost in shoe stores, real-estate offices, and insurance agencies."

Boeing may be taken as an example of the defense industry's problems — even though that company's business today is four-fifths commercial. In 1970 alone, Boeing's total sales expanded by more than $840 million, to $3.7 billion, but defense revenues declined by 25 percent. This decline, coupled with a high learning curve on defense projects and rising costs, forced Boeing to reduce its total work force in 1970 from around 110,000 to around 50,000 — probably some kind of record. Yet even that reduction barely kept Boeing out of the red. On its enormous $3.7-billion volume it had a niggardly operating net of $4,800,-000.

Space and defense contractors, when they contemplate such happenings, understandably find it hard to demonstrate a vast enthusiasm about their future. Some have been diversifying into commercial products, and many more are looking around. But the most important question for most of them still concerns military and space procurement. Will it rise with G.N.P.? Or will it stay at around $40 billion? Or will it decline still more?

A complex threat

Nobody can say for sure. But it seems at least to be clear that the new antiwar attitudes, rooted in new values and new ways of thinking about social problems, will be exerting powerful pressures to hold down defense spending in the years ahead. The new attitudes are pervasive; many Americans today believe sincerely that the U.S. is menaced by no threat so grave as its own military-industrial complex. This complex, the subject of a tremendous outpouring of books and articles in the last few years, is said to be an elite consisting of the Pentagon, industrialists, legislators, labor leaders, and reactionary academicians, all aiming at global expansion and promoting war by championing excessive preparations for it. Some of these arguments seem almost paranoid, and restrained versions of them sound fairly extreme by most standards.

Consider, for example, the proposals of Professor Seymour Melman of Columbia, a long-time critic of the military and author of the bitter tract *Pentagon Capitalism: The Political Economy of War.* Melman maintains that the defense budget could be slashed *by* — not to — around $50 billion. Outlays of around $25 billion at today's prices, Melman argues, would be enough to operate an adequate strategic deterrent force, guard the shores of the U.S., and participate in international peace-keeping operations. The figures seem incredible to most students of the subject, but Melman's thesis did seem plausible to many, including several eminent members of Congress. At a 1969 conference on the military budget and national priorities, Senators Fulbright, McGovern, Nelson, Hughes, and Mondale were among those signing a report plunking for a $50-billion cut. (It is doubtful they all would do so today.)

Even if these extreme assaults on defense spending are held off, some significant spending cuts may yet be proposed. In its August 1, 1969, issue *Fortune* explored the case for some cuts. The military budget, *Fortune* concluded, was getting out of control, and could be considerably reduced without sacrificing any of the armed forces' effectiveness. It suggested a post-Vietnam budget of about $61 billion, the result of cuts totaling $17.6 billion, mostly achieved by reducing the general-purpose (as distinguished from strategic nuclear) forces. Such a budget would afford scant comfort to defense contractors. In constant 1971 dollars, it would imply procurement outlays of something between $30 billion and $35 billion, depending on the existing ratio of procurement to wage and operating expenses. So even with a generous allowance for space outlays, the space and military contractors, at least for several years, would find themselves with a market of considerably less than $40 billion.

Some other serious proposals would shrink the market further. Early in 1971 the National Urban Coalition published an ambitious and challenging book entitled *Counterbudget: A Blueprint for Changing National Priorities.* The blueprint envisages reducing the military budget to $60.2 billion in fiscal 1972 and then to around $50 billion from 1973 through 1976. With such levels of expenditures, procurement might account for a larger percentage of total outlays than it does now. But even so, and given a generous space budget, the space and military contract market would fall far short of $35 billion.

This proposal is no arbitrary one. Its author, who was director of the counterbudget project, is Robert Benson, who served in the controller's department in the Pentagon. In preparing his thesis Benson enjoyed the advice and help of, among others, Charles Schultze, former director of the U.S. budget, and Robert Anthony, former controller of the Department of Defense (and now professor of management control at the Harvard Business School). Benson shunned the D.O.D.'s usual procedure of beginning with the previous budget and working forward (usually upward) from there, and instead started "from the bottom up." He reanalyzed the job defense is supposed to do, estimated what it would take to counter the expected threat, and then synthesized a budget.

In general, Benson found himself disputing the need for large forces and many complex and sophisticated weapons. He decided the U.S. strategic force, whose purpose is to deter nuclear attack, is more than big enough to absorb an enemy blow and still strike back devastatingly; in fact he concluded that *each* of the three deterrents — Polaris submarines, Minuteman land-based missiles, and B-52 and FB-111 bombers — is itself sufficient for the job. His plan calls for strengthening the underwater deterrence by continuing to convert Polaris submarines to Poseidons, and laying out more money for the ULMS (underwater long-range missile system). In return, Benson argues, work should stop on various projects, including Minuteman improvement, and development of a new B-1 bomber; and most of the B-52 bombers and the air-defense system should be phased out. All

The Defense Industry's Declining Share of Defense

Defense spending has been falling in recent years, and the decline has been concentrated in procurement — i.e., in sales by companies identifiable as "the defense industry." Between the 1968 and 1972 fiscal years, procurement will have declined by 20 percent, from $45.4 billion to an estimated $36.4 billion, or from 58 to 48 percent of total defense outlays. In constant dollars, a better measure of the physical volume of purchases, procurement will be off around 31 percent.

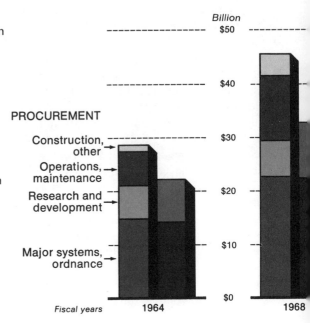

Billion

PROCUREMENT

Construction, other →
Operations, → maintenance
Research and → development

Major systems, → ordnance

$50
$40
$30
$20
$10
$0

Fiscal years   1964   1968

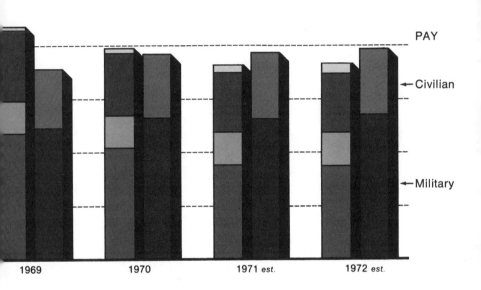

PAY

←Civilian

←Military

1969   1970   1971 *est.*   1972 *est.*

this would save nearly $6 billion in strategic outlays. Cuts in general-purpose or conventional forces would save $15 billion more. Attack-carrier fleets, for example, could be reduced from twelve to seven, saving $450 million annually on each task force. Another $5 billion would be saved by ending the war in Indochina.

Sizing up the Russians

But all this, plausible as it sounds, runs up against the second great uncertainty hounding military contractors. Just what are the underlying realities of our strategic situation? How much will it take to contain the threat? As Benson himself puts it, "The crux of the matter is the definition of the systems required to contain the threat," and there happen to be a lot of plausible definitions around. Even Lawrence Lynn Jr., professor of business economics at Stanford and former Administration consultant who advocates lean military spending, remarks that the counterbudget program, aside from being "hopelessly unattainable politically," is too low.

The view that the threat is substantial begins with the finding that the Soviet Union itself, as a closed society, is one big proudly aggressive military-industrial complex. What the Soviet military establishment plausibly says it needs, it gets by fiat. Nobody asks the Russian people about it, and indeed nobody would think of telling them about it. Soviet newspaper columnists do not palaver endlessly about the nation's strategy, and Soviet trade papers do not report its new and proposed weaponry in minute detail. Not even the Supreme Soviet, periodically assembled in its proletarian majesty, discusses Russian military needs in any more depth or detail than is necessary to rubber-stamp them.

Confronted with a threat so formidable looking, the American military establishment feels it would be derelict in its duty if it did not at least tend to err, if err it must, on the side of ordering too much rather than too little. That is why it is leery of any proposals that seem to involve just scraping by. When Admiral Thomas H. Moorer, Chairman of the Joint Chiefs of Staff, presented the military's argument before Congress last March, he was plainly making the best of his case, but he was not dissembling. The mutual ability of the Soviet Union and the U.S. to destroy each other, he has maintained, is not itself a solution to our defense problems; for Soviet superiority in ground forces would still undermine U.S. diplomacy by destroying the world's confidence in the ability of the U.S. to wage any kind of war except one of mutual extermination. And now, Moorer told Congress gloomily, even the *strategic* balance has shifted dramatically in favor of the Soviet Union, and the comfortable U.S. lead has all but vanished.

Moorer's pessimism was considerably fortified by the tidings that the Soviet Union was constructing silos for new intercontinental ballistic missiles that may be even larger and more powerful than its SS-9's. Some experts have already described these new installations as a definite move toward a first-strike capability. Moorer did not go quite so far, but he did recommend such measures as improving the ability of Minuteman silos to withstand attacking missiles, development of a prototype antimissile system to augment the Safeguard defense around Minuteman complexes, and development of new bomber bases, dispersed inland.

An exchange of freezes

The catch to any such moves is that they might reinforce fears that the U.S. was moving toward a first-strike capability. Those who are skeptical about a massive Soviet threat tend, in general, to fear that our own buildups will seem provocative to the Russians. They have pointed, for example, to the fact that the U.S. has designed a hard-target killing accuracy into the Poseidon — an accuracy not needed to preserve our second-strike capability

Dr. Foster and the case for superiority

Perhaps no man has more to say about what military contracting will be like in the years ahead than John Foster Jr., forty-nine, who has been director of research and engineering in the Department of Defense since 1965. Dr. Foster is a man with a mission, devoted single-mindedly to containing the threat. The term refers not merely to the military potential of the Soviet Union but to its research and development. Says Foster: "It is absolutely essential that the free world be technologically superior to the Soviet Union. There is no room here for parity."

To many, this view of the case may seem arbitrary, but to Foster it is elementary logic. The nature and approximate schedules of all important U.S. weapon systems now under development are well known to our friends and our enemies, but the military laboratories and research centers of the Soviet Union and Warsaw Pact nations are shrouded in secrecy. The free world's only possible offset to this secrecy is technological superiority. Such superiority is not merely a matter of introducing new weapons, Foster argues, but of making continuous progress in the basic technologies of weaponry. By 1974, he "safely" predicts, the U.S. will once again be given pause by Soviet achievements in both military and space technology.

In principle, even many critics of arms spending concede that military R. and D. should not be stinted. In practice, however, it has been dropping both in real terms and in relation to Soviet R. and D. There was a plateau in U.S. spending between 1953 and 1957; but after the launching of Sputnik, U.S. military R. and D. outlays soared and overtook those of the U.S.S.R. In the late 1960's U.S. spending leveled off at around $7.5 billion, while Soviet outlays rose steadily and unobtrusively; they are now about $10 billion. Unless the U.S. decides soon to increase its outlays, this gap will widen enormously throughout the 1970's. Owing to inflation, even a level funding of military R. and D. during the next five years would mean something like a 5 to 8 percent annual decline in real effort. By 1975, Foster believes, we should add about $5 billion to the current level.

He concedes that there may be ways to spend our R. and D. funds more efficiently. One way would be for NATO members to get together and weed out the overlaps in their programs. Another would be for the Pentagon to re-examine all its own programs with the same idea in mind. Even so, Foster says, "I do not believe that our present programs and level of effort, even with the most we can realize in improved management, can match the threat. . . . We must have the support of the American people."

against the SS-9's. This could provoke a major Soviet response. Because both sides may have a case, the Strategic Arms Limitation Talks (SALT) at Vienna have sometimes bogged down. The U.S. doubts that Soviet leadership has really accepted the concept of strategic sufficiency; the Soviet Union appears to be worrying that the Safeguard antimissile system could be expanded to cover most of the U.S. and that this expansion in effect could be a move toward a first-strike capacity. Senator Henry Jackson of the state of Washington has proposed that the Soviet Union freeze its offensive missile buildup in return for a freeze in the American deployment of Minuteman III missiles with MIRV warheads. But the Soviet Union is not likely to cooperate unless the U.S. does something about Poseidon as well as Minuteman III. Senator Hubert Humphrey has suggested that we might resolve this impasse by seeking an agreement banning or limiting all ABM systems; and he has also called upon Congress to hold up money for MIRV missiles and to ask the Soviet Union to show similar restraint.

The most that can be expected of SALT is an agreement to trade off a ceiling on the number of SS-9's for one on the Safeguard, perhaps even a ban on further deployment of all offensive and defensive weapons by both sides. This, of course, would be a lot, and would tend to keep arms spending down. But even such an agreement probably would not end the arms race. As the Federation of American Scientists has warned, it could become "an umbrella" under which the race could continue with qualitative improvements.

Why competition means high costs

And if there is no SALT agreement, the arms race might be stepped up considerably. A good many defense contractors who have studied the strategic situation closely are convinced not only that the nation's defensive ability is eroding, but that it is only a matter of time before Congress thinks so. "I have to be-

lieve," says Jack Parker, vice chairman of General Electric, "that
in a couple of years the gap will be so apparent that Senators
McGovern and Proxmire will feel we should be doing something
different."

Even those who agree about the threat may disagree about
appropriate levels of defense spending. Since the level of spending is not, of course, determined by the normal constraints of the
marketplace, some disagreements are inevitable. Military weapons are capital goods, but they are capital goods with no economic use and needing no economic justification. In the universe
inhabited by civilians it might be possible to build a kitchen machine that would call up the grocer, do the cooking, wash dishes,
and perhaps even wait on tables; but there would be no market
for such machines because nobody could afford them. The military is under no such constraint. Whatever is technologically
possible, provided it promises to improve performance, is
deemed useful and may be bought. Competition spurs the military not to get things done more cheaply, but to outdo the competitor threat at any cost.

Consequently its devices have been growing immensely complex and expensive, even aside from the effects of inflation.
A Navy F-4 fighter currently costs $3 million; its heir apparent
will cost a lot more; the total might go as high as $20 million
apiece when the plane is completely equipped. The Sturgeon
class submarine set the government back $80 million, but the
new SSN-688 nuclear sub will come to at least $160 million. The
M-60 tank, which has been produced since 1959, lists at around
$176,000; the new XM-803 was ticketed at about $1 million until
Deputy Defense Secretary David Packard cut it down to $600,-
000.

It may well be, as some critics argue, that the Pentagon is
overstressing advanced performance in some weapon systems —
demanding in tactical aircraft, for example, more speed, range,
fire accuracy, "loiter" time, and bomb load than is needed. In
any event, it is clear that many weapons tend to be overexpen-
sive, and sometimes, as in the case of the unlucky F-111, too
complex to be entirely reliable. The Soviet Union is often said to

prefer simpler and cheaper planes and weapons, but there seem to be a fair number of exceptions to the rule. According to Robert Perry of the Rand Corp., the Russian mach 3 fighter is at least as complex as the U.S. F-14.

The cost of weapon systems already approved but still to be produced probably runs to more than $100 billion. In addition, dozens of weapon systems have received only preliminary approvals. One, calculated to replace the B-52, is the B-1 supersonic long-range bomber now being developed by North American Rockwell. Although the B-1 was originally estimated to cost $30 million a copy, the Pentagon will be lucky to get it for $50 million. The craft is under considerable attack as being unnecessary in a missile age, and its fate probably will not be known until North American Rockwell finishes three prototypes.

If the weaponry and systems that have received only preliminary approval are added to prospective outlays, the total might come to $200 billion over the next decade or so; that would imply procurement outlays perhaps $4 billion or $5 billion a year above present levels. It is certainly possible that not all the weapon systems will be approved, and that many orders will be cut back. Recently, for example, the Air Force shaved the final F-111 order from 82 to 70 aircraft. (When the military first contracted for the F-111, it expected to order more than 1,700. It will actually buy only 526.) No one knows the extent to which congressionally imposed cutbacks will shrink that $200 billion.

The road from cost-plus

Another large uncertainty about the totals resides in the procurement process itself. Having been investigated, exposed, and intensively denounced for some two years, the process looks as if it would almost certainly be overhauled. That an overhaul is needed nobody denies. The biggest and most characteristic defect of military procurement is that the government all too often finds itself paying much more for defense systems than it had projected or contracted for.

Secretary McNamara tried to get both more competition and an early fix on costs into the procurement process. To keep costs down, he discouraged cost-plus-fixed-fee contracts and introduced incentives. But this quest for certitude just didn't work in the early development stages of advanced weapon systems. The Pentagon often felt obliged to start production before all development problems were solved, and it often changed specifications after production had started. So contractors found themselves with "cost growths" and "overruns" that the government had to pay for. Often the contractor's initial estimate was manifestly much too low; dearly wanting the business, the company "bought into it." Even when the military suspected or knew the estimate was low, it often picked up the bid simply because it was eager to get the program going. A good example was Lockheed's almost fatally low bid for the C-5 military transport.

Meanwhile, the traditional cost-plus contract still has its problems. Fees are calculated as a percentage of the estimated cost of the program, a standard, blameless practice. But the main problem about the cost-plus contract is that the contractor often uses government-owned tools and machinery and draws down government progress payments. Thus the percentage return on his own equity capital can get up to staggering levels. If the contract provides for a fixed fee, moreover, a contractor who does a poor job sometimes makes out as well financially as one who performs efficiently. Says Ivan Selin, former head of systems management in the Pentagon, "The incentives are all wrong. The Defense Department guarantees you a little money, no matter how bad you are, rather than let you make a lot of money if you are good. It doesn't care how much you spend so long as no one seems to get too much profit."

The imperfections in procurement have been dwelt on extensively by the redoubtable Senator William Proxmire and his subcommittee (of the Joint Economic Committee) on economy in government. Nothing even vaguely suspicious has escaped the sharp scrutiny of Proxmire and his assistants. "This year," Proxmire boasted in 1969, "is the year that Congress and the American taxpayer found out about cost overruns in military procurement." Moreover, the subcommittee's able economist, Richard Kaufman, used the material uncovered by the committee in a book, *The War Profiteers*, published in February 1971. Perhaps to boost his own profits, Kaufman somewhat sensationalized his material. Some of his examples of profiteering are impossible to verify satisfactorily. He implies that everybody who sells to the Pentagon makes excessive profits on invested capital, but the general case is that space and military contractors make much less on government work than on commercial work. Kaufman does, however, provide quite a few examples of the well-known tendency for men in high technology to underestimate rather than overestimate costs; his examples also make it clear that the profit motive performs its classical job of restraining costs only when there is competition, and that monopoly in government, like monopoly anywhere else, inevitably results in abuse.

A dispute about equity

Some of the concerns registered by the Proxmire subcommittee are shared in the executive branch. In June 1969, President Nixon appointed a blue-ribbon defense panel under Gilbert Fitzhugh, chairman of the board of Metropolitan Life Insurance Co., to look into the operations of the D.O.D. The panel found plenty wrong, and said so bluntly. It recommended nothing less than a thorough reorganization of the department, including its procurement policies.

Finally, the General Accounting Office, needled by Proxmire, has made its own investigation of procurement profits. Its report, released in March 1971, included the results of a questionnaire sent to the largest contractors. Between 1966 and 1969, seventy-four of these contractors said, they had realized an average pre-tax profit of 4.3 percent on D.O.D. sales, against 9.9 percent on commercial sales; they also reported that their return on equity capital (i.e., capital employed in both D.O.D. and commercial work) was about 22 percent. The return-on-capital data got to be a controversial matter; in the same report the G.A.O. itself quarreled with some of these data. In a study of 146 completed contracts worth $4.3 billion, the organization found that average earnings on equity capital were no less than 56 percent.

Now, as already noted, return on equity capital can be a deceptive measure. And while Senator Proxmire hailed the G.A.O.'s finding, Controller Elmer Staats, the organization's chief official, said the 146 contracts were not representative, and David Packard agreed. Packard did, however, allow that the high level of progress payments makes for an "unhealthy contracting situation."

The mills of Pentagon reform grind slowly. In general, the Pentagon seems to be paying some attention to the recommendations of the Fitzhugh report. It also seems to be impressed by the views of Assistant Treasury Secretary Murray Weidenbaum, a close student of military contracting. Weidenbaum, for instance, wants defense contractors to use their own capital instead of depending on government equipment and progress payments; he also believes they should diversify further into civilian lines.

For his part, David Packard has reintroduced a "fly before you buy" policy that puts early development and design work on a cost-plus basis. Only after the development work is done — after the plane flies, so to speak — are production contracts to be let; whenever possible, these are to involve a fixed price. Packard is also encouraging the competitive development of prototypes; Fairchild Hiller and Northrop, for example, are both developing the A-X ground-support craft.

Packard has announced he is delegating more authority to the officers in charge of major weapon development. Major General Douglas Nelson, who was assigned the $1.4-billion supersonic B-1 development program, recently took the initiative by deciding to save both time and money by shrinking the initial stages of the program; instead of five planes for flight and two for ground testing, North American Rockwell will build three and one. In

the renegotiated contract, the program will come to perhaps
$300 million less than the original deal. That happens to be fine
with North American Rockwell, for it augurs a better chance of
congressional approval and a quicker decision on production,
which is where the money, if any, will be.

It is symptomatic of the widespread dissatisfaction with
present procurement arrangements that there has recently been
talk of nationalizing big defense contractors or forming one big
nonprofit corporation to handle primary contracts. No such extreme proposals seem to have much chance. What may and
should have a chance is a proposal advanced by Charles
Schultze before the Proxmire subcommittee in 1969. Arguing
that perhaps the most important reason for runaway military
budgets was that major decisions are rarely subjected to outside
review and discussion, Schultze recommended that the Secretary
of State submit an annual "posture statement" to Congress, out-
lining the nation's overseas commitments, and that the D.O.D.
"posture statement" then incorporate a five-year projection of
defense expenditures. Furthermore, said Schultze, "an appropriate institution" in Congress, perhaps a new joint committee,
should be empowered to review and analyze these "posture
statements," and Congress itself should issue a report on them.
Proxmire is among those who support the idea.

How Raytheon did it

In firming up and rationalizing the rules of the game, the Pentagon will somewhat reduce the uncertainties that now envelop
defense contracting. But it is hard to envisage any reforms that
would still leave most big contractors sanguine about the defense industry's basic prospects. When the military market was
booming and money was no object, they were not very enthusi-
astic about expanding into commercial work. But these days the
defense game seems triply precarious. First, there are probably
too many companies in the business; second, there are dangers of

still further cutbacks — and when the government cuts back, it does so with a meat ax; and third, profits on individual contracts, which have rarely lived up to the much-publicized opportunities for "profiteering," are even less likely to do so now. Thus there is now a good deal of talk in the defense industry about mergers and diversification, and even that some large defense contractors will get out of the business entirely. Says Packard: "We have an entire defense industry somewhat larger than we will be needing in the next five to ten years. The base is already shrinking, and there may be some opportunities and some need for mergers." Robert Anthony, who was the Pentagon's controller during part of the Johnson Administration, also feels that the industry is overpopulated. If defense spending rose only enough to offset inflation, he believes, then one of the big contractors would be likely to depart the industry. If the budget got down to the $50-billion level, two or three major contractors might get out.

For a few companies, diversification is an old story. Back in 1964, when government work accounted for more than 80 percent of its turnover, Raytheon decided that the time had come to think of other things. Using its experience with military radar, it developed its profitable Radarange microwave home-kitchen oven. Then it bought more than a dozen companies, among them Caloric Corp., the kitchen-equipment maker, and Amana Refrigeration Inc. These ventures have prospered to the point where Raytheon's defense sales are down to half of the total. And in 1970, a bad year in the defense business, its sales and profits were only a shade below their all-time high.

Another shining example of diversification out of defense is Rohr Corp., a California "metal-bending" outfit with a $288-million stake in making jet-engine housings or pods. Competing against established professionals like Pullman-Standard and St. Louis Car, Rohr recently landed a $67-million contract for building cars for the new San Francisco Bay Area rapid-transit line.

Boeing has recently announced a major diversification program. The company says that it confidently looks forward to the day when the aerospace business will be booming again, but that it has nevertheless decided to broaden its base; ten years from now a third of Boeing's sales may be outside aerospace. Among the ventures the company has considered are surface transportation and community development.

The problem of shifting to sewage

Other defense companies, noting Rohr's initial success, and also noting predictions that someday the Transportation Department will be spending twice as much on urban transportation as NASA now spends on space, are eying the surface-transportation market too. But the market may not be as easy to crack as it looks, says A. Scheffer Lang, head of the transportation systems division of the Department of Civil Engineering at M.I.T. For one thing, not much money is yet available, and until the government mounts a major program, it's not likely to be. For another, Lang says, "Companies that have been built around D.O.D. and NASA contracting are just downright inept in dealing with the uncertainties of a commercial market. Their engineering approach relies heavily on dollar overkill as the way to solve problems."

Out of all the tribulations besetting space and military procurement, however, at least one consensus may arise. Nothing has so aroused the concern of contractors, the military, and Congressmen as the way in which procurement cutbacks have summarily dumped legions of trained engineers and scientists onto the unemployed lists. Able, even brilliant men who have devoted years to a valuable and rare specialty have found themselves unemployable. "Politically, it's one thing to say we should divert our efforts to ecology," says Henry Singleton, chairman of Teledyne. "But a man who has worked on defense usually can't do that. You can't send a man with thirty years' experience as a radar expert to work on sewage treatment. It takes a generation to shift to sewage."

Almost to a man, defense contractors argue that procurement

cuts, when necessary, should be made gradually, and that the Pentagon must agree on a consistent long-term defense program that will not be hit by sudden expansions or contractions except in emergencies. It doesn't seem like too much to ask.

Six

Capital Goods
May Get a Growing Share

Some familiar relationships between capital and output have changed surprisingly in recent years, and the plant and equipment market in the 1970's may swell as a result.

During much of the past decade U.S. business was on a tremendous capital-investment spree — one whose only real precedent in modern times was the burst of investment that followed World War II. Private spending for capital goods more than doubled in 1961–69: the rise was from $47 billion a year to $99.3 billion. Some of that gain represents inflation, of course, but even in real terms, i.e., eliminating the effects of price increases, capital spending rose by 78 percent during those years. That works out to an average annual increase of 7½ percent, a breathtaking pace to sustain over so long a period.

The capital-investment spree was an essential ingredient of the business boom of the 1960's, the longest in U.S. history. And the decline in capital spending was an important element in last year's broad business setback. Spending in real terms will almost certainly be down in 1971 too, which is one reason the economy seems unlikely to soar this year. A full recovery would require capital investment to come back strongly.

Gauging its ability to do so raises a question about that investment performance of the 1960's. Must it be viewed as a unique and special event — or one that might, with variations, be repeated? Right now there is some dispute about whether the causes of the boom really were so "special"; some economists, at least, are coming to believe that the causes involved some longer-run changes that might mean sustained high levels of capital spending.

In particular, the course of the recent spending spree, which went well beyond what most economists had forecast, left many of them feeling that they were suddenly confronting new questions about the way capital-investment decisions are made. Why,

Portrait of an Explosion

Capital spending grew rather modestly in the 1950's and early 1960's, as the large chart at right shows. The great boom in spending did not gather momentum until 1963, but soon thereafter it began to soar for several different reasons. One was the widespread desire of business to beat the increasing inflation in costs. That increase is expressed here by the widening gap between the lines for expenditures in current and in constant dollars. Note that spending in constant dollars declined in 1970.

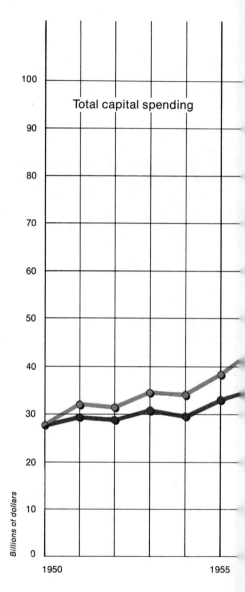

Total capital spending

Billions of dollars

100

90

80

70

60

50

40

30

20

10

0

1950   1955

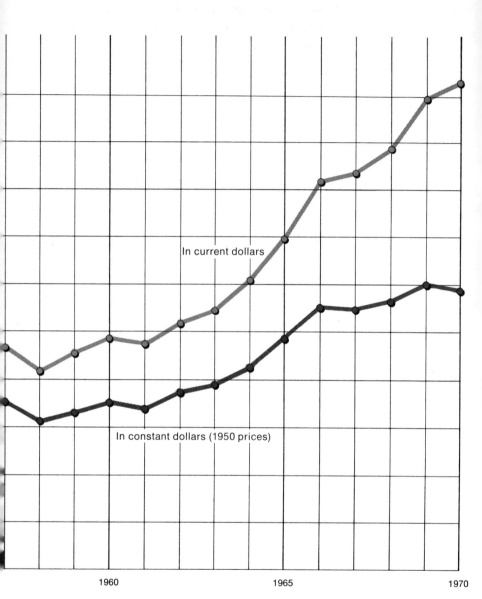

In current dollars

In constant dollars (1950 prices)

1960   1965   1970

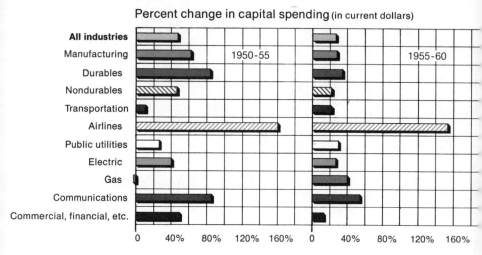

Percent change in capital spending (in current dollars)

	1950-55	1955-60
All industries		
Manufacturing		
Durables		
Nondurables		
Transportation		
Airlines		
Public utilities		
Electric		
Gas		
Communications		
Commercial, financial, etc.		

0 40% 80% 120% 160% 0 40% 80% 120% 160%

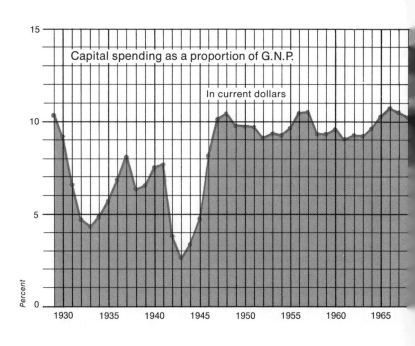

Capital spending as a proportion of G.N.P.

In current dollars

Percent

15

10

5

0

1930 1935 1940 1945 1950 1955 1960 1965

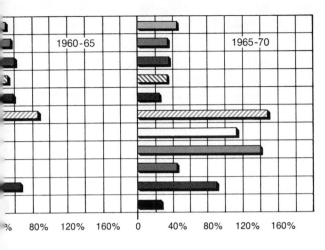

| 1960-65 | 1965-70 |

%   80%   120%   160%   0   40%   80%   120%   160%

The horizontal bars show that the boom was most unevenly
distributed over the U.S. economy. Spending by airlines has
led that of other industries in every five-year period shown;
however, spending by the total transportation group (which
also includes railroads and trucking) has grown only modestly.
The industries represented here account for about 80 percent of all capital investment.

Capital spending as a proportion of G.N.P. (chart at left)
fell badly in the depression and during World War II. After
the war it rarely exceeded 10 percent until the mid-1960's;
but starting in 1965 the figure topped 10 percent for six
years, averaging 10.5 percent (versus the 9.6 percent average of 1947-64). Several economists believe the new level is
here to stay or may rise. They believe capital has become
less efficient or is being used less efficiently, or that there
are new needs for heavy capital spending — e.g., for pollution controls.

for example, were appropriations in manufacturing at such high levels in 1968–69, when the use of productive facilities was declining? Was chronic inflation inducing businessmen to make capital-investment decisions in new ways? Was capital becoming less efficient (as some economists suspect)?

Business investment, however, will also be affected by the large new uncertainties that hang over the U.S. economy as a whole. These new uncertainties have been elaborated in previous articles in this series. There is, for example, the possibility that new "antimaterialist" values might seriously restrain growth in the years ahead; conceivably, they might even culminate in policies explicitly renouncing economic growth as a national objective. Any such developments would plainly have devastating effects on capital spending.

Finally, all the concerns about the environment are raising questions about the capital equipment that will be needed to hold down pollution. This particular issue will be dealt with in the next chapter.

What, then, can be said about the prospects for capital spending during the 1970's? Perhaps the best way to begin answering the question is with the most elementary of statements: the level of capital spending will depend on (*a*) the level of output and (*b*) the capital-output ratio (which meaures the amount of plant and equipment needed per unit of output).

A swing of half a trillion

Possible variations in the level of output in the 1970's are immense. Most projections of the economy assume that "normal" growth during the decade will raise output by something like 4.3 percent a year. But the elements underlying that assumption are very much open to question. The main elements are growth of the labor force and growth in productivity. Their sum may indeed come to an average of about 4.3 percent a year in the decade ahead, but the uncertainties about each of them are large enough so that it is easy to arrive at much lower and much higher possibilities. It was suggested in chapter 1 that a quite plausible range of growth rates for the decade would be from $2\frac{1}{2}$ percent to about $5\frac{3}{4}$ percent. The range between the low and high growth rates involves a difference approaching $500 billion in 1980 output (in 1970 prices).

On balance, it appears that the new values taking hold in the U.S. are doing more to slow economic growth than to accelerate it. Some consequences of these new values are discernible in the news from many different parts of the U.S. Many states and communities are becoming more selective, even in a period of rising unemployment, about the kinds of business they are trying to draw. Growth in general seems less attractive: the Los Angeles City Planning Commission is now considering a rezoning that would allow for a future population of five (rather than ten) million by the year 2020. Even though much of its livelihood depends on coal, West Virginia feels impelled to limit strip mining. The new Disney World in Orlando, Florida, is not receiving a wholehearted welcome. Power companies in many areas of the country are finding it difficult to get permits to build new generating plants.

The consequences for capital spending of a significant reduction in economic growth are, within limits, quite predictable. As the chart on page 124 shows, capital spending has always been close to 10 percent of gross national product in the postwar period; in no year has it been less than 9 percent or more than 11 percent of G.N.P. Thus questions about capital spending in 1980 must begin with that $500-billion "swing" in G.N.P. It would seem to imply a difference on the order of $50 billion in the annual level of capital investment by the end of the decade.

A *rather elusive ratio*

The consequences of a change in the capital-output ratio are harder to get at — in part because the ratio itself is a rather elusive matter. One part of the problem has to do with the difficulty of getting an agreed-upon figure for it. The "output" part of the ratio is, of course, the G.N.P. But how much "capital" is there in the U.S. these days?

Some economists have defined capital as the total book value of all private equipment and structures (except housing). Some start with an estimate of all facilities in place at some point in the past and calculate the flow of replacements and additions to them. The Commerce Department's Office of Business Economics, using this method, has estimated that the gross private capital stock of the U.S. in 1969 was $925 billion (in 1958 prices). It is also possible to use a "net" concept of the capital stock, i.e., by depreciating it; the O.B.E. has calculated that, on a straight-line basis, the depreciated private stock in 1969 was $532 billion (again, in 1958 prices). Economists are agreed that the capital-output ratio is a very important matter, but the difficulty of arriving at one simple, unambiguous figure has led many of them to prefer to discuss it in somewhat general terms — i.e., to concentrate their analyses on the direction of changes in the ratio rather than on its absolute value. At times economists use the proportion of capital spending to G.N.P. as a convenient "proxy" for the ratio.

There is at least no doubt why the ratio is important — or why a permanent change in the proportion of G.N.P. going to capital spending would be a momentous event. For while the proportion has remained in that seemingly narrow band between 9 and 11 percent in the postwar period, swings within that range have massive effects on the economy. In the years from 1947 to 1964, the proportion of capital spending to G.N.P. averaged 9.6 percent. But from 1965 to 1970 the average was 10.5 percent. In a trillion-dollar economy, that difference of nine-tenths of 1 percent added $9 billion to capital spending.

It is, of course, usual for the proportion to bounce around from year to year, but for it to stay at a new high plateau for as long as six years is most unusual. To some economists the sequence of events has suggested the possibility that the capital-output ratio has been permanently affected, and that some established economic wisdom now needs to be revised.

The established wisdom, based on a considerable historical record, takes it as "given" that the capital-output ratio tends to decline over the long run. The reason is that new capital is almost always more efficient than the capital it supplements or replaces. It is this proposition that is now in question. After a recent exhaustive analysis of data on capital stocks and output, economists at the National Planning Association have concluded that the efficiency of capital may actually have been falling. They believe that the requirements for additional pollution controls will ensure further declines in efficiency (which would mean further rises in the capital-output ratio).

Some students of the subject have cited other reasons why more capital may be needed now to produce a given volume of goods and services. Economic consultant Alan Greenspan has commented that "companies in a number of industries are more interested in marketing their production than in seeking adequate rates of return on their investments"; in other words, some recent spending should not have taken place at all or should have been directed elsewhere. Whatever the motives of those who make the spending decisions, it is at least clear that a good deal of recent capital investment has had a low payoff. For example, Edwin H. Gott, chairman of U.S. Steel, has complained that "despite our enlarged and expensive program to acquire better tools of production over the past five years, there is no evidence that we are experiencing the higher rates of productivity that all of these new facilities are designed to give us."

A question about work

The performance of labor as well as management may be involved in the reduced efficiency of some kinds of capital. Younger workers and senior management have quite different notions about work discipline — indeed, about work. Whether the

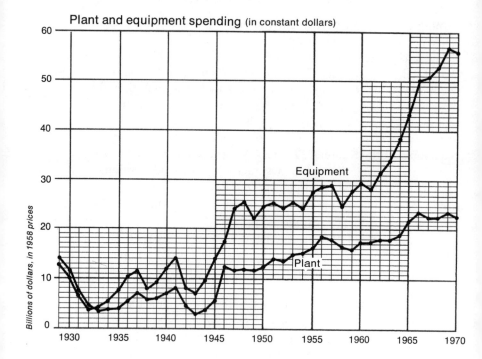

Plant and equipment spending (in constant dollars)

Billions of dollars, in 1958 prices

Equipment

Plant

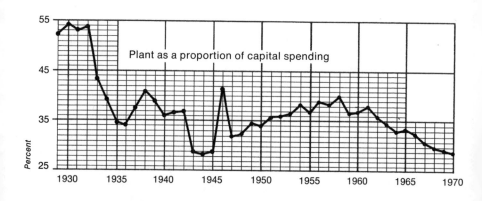

Plant as a proportion of capital spending

Percent

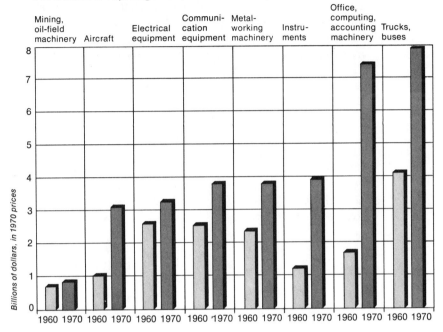

Purchases of capital goods (in constant dollars)

Where the Money Went

There have been several distinct changes in the structure of capital spending in the past forty years. As the top chart at left shows, spending on plant lagged behind spending on equipment (both measured in constant dollars) from 1930 to 1945. From 1945 through 1960, outlays for plant actually grew somewhat faster than those for equipment. Thereafter a huge gap in favor of equipment opened up. One major element causing the gap: the costs of plant construction have risen roughly 50 percent since 1960, versus 20 percent for equipment.

Recent trends in purchases of several varieties of equipment are shown in the chart above. Equipment associated with automation, such as computers and instruments, has gained the most. Purchases of aircraft have tripled; those of trucks and buses have doubled.

less authoritarian forms of supervision that seem bound to prevail in future years will yield more output per man-hour in the long run, or whether they will drive management to replace workers with machinery faster than usual, is one of the major uncertainties about the capital-goods market. The trend to a four-day week is another. Nobody today knows with any assurance what widespread adoption of the four-day week — in either the thirty-two- or forty-hour version — would do to the demand for capital.

Economists in General Electric's forecasting service are among those who agree that the capital-output ratio is rising. However, their reasoning is different from that of economists projecting a general decline in the efficiency of capital. The G.E. group expects the ratio to rise for several special reasons, including a relative increase in spending by capital-intensive industries, e.g., utilities.

Still another reason for anticipating that the capital-output ratio will remain at a high level has been advanced by George Terborgh, an economist long associated with the Machinery and Allied Products Institute. Terborgh has put forward a quite ingenious explanation of the recent boom in investment. He thinks that much of the "extra" spending was related to a speedup in the average annual growth of the labor force — the growth rate rose from less than 1 percent a year to 1.6 percent during 1965–70 — and also to the reduction in unemployment that went on during most of the 1960's. The resulting large increase in total employment, Terborgh argues, required unusually high capital outlays simply to "support" the average worker in the style to which U.S. industry is accustomed: on the average, industry invests $15,000 per man nowadays. Terborgh calculates that the extra employment accounts for most of the extra investment of the late 1960's. He believes that rapid labor-force growth in the 1970's will continue to stimulate capital spending.

A plausible case can be made, however, that the recent increase in the capital-output ratio is only temporary. For example, in the paper, chemical, steel, and electric-power industries, companies seem to have been spending in especially large chunks recently by building huge plants or investing in radically new kinds of technology; in either case, the payoff, in increased output per dollar of investment, might simply be delayed — i.e., until the longer than usual "shakedown" period associated with such projects finally ends. Moreover, the installation of very large primary producing plants often requires a host of additions to fabricating, finishing, or transmission facilities that may then become temporarily excessive in relation to the amount of primary output. The whole process works to depress efficiency until a balance is restored.

It also seems likely that the special investment demands of a few industries have worked to increase the capital-spending totals temporarily. Spending by airlines increased sevenfold from 1963 through 1970 as they bought four-motored jets, then rounded out their fleets with two- and three-motor versions, and more recently began to add the jumbo 747's. As a result, they were also forced to enlarge and improve their ground facilities. And in communications, continued growth in ordinary telephone usage, combined with the large increases in data transmission that accompanied the spread of computerization, created tremendous demand for more sophisticated switching gear as well as for microwave equipment and coaxial cables.

Another special influence working to raise capital outlays was a series of changes in tax and depreciation laws. For example, an investment credit of 7 percent was instituted in 1962 and corporate income taxes were cut in 1964. Even though the credit was temporarily suspended in 1966–67 and rescinded by 1970, both measures were stimulating outlays over much of the decade. Such changes commonly have delayed effects, and they were probably still at work toward the end of the period. (Economist Dale Jorgenson of Harvard has calculated that it takes more than a year for changes in depreciation practices to increase capital spending, and he believes that the maximum impact may not be felt for at least four years.) A new set of liberalized rules for taking depreciation have been adopted, the latest in a series of reforms stretching back to 1954. Each liberalization adds another fraction to the profitability of capital, and as

M.I.T.'s Paul Samuelson puts it, "All those little numbers working all night long add up."

Tracking down the inflation

Perhaps the most common explanation for the apparent rise in the capital-output ratio in recent years is that businessmen have speeded up their purchases of plant and equipment in an effort to beat inflation — i.e., capital put in place today will be cheaper than capital put in place tomorrow. The explanation has a lot of common sense going for it, and in addition it appears to be supported by the performances of a number of econometric models. In general, the models used to forecast capital outlays were underestimating expenditures in the late 1960's. As the results got further and further out of line, some economists — for example, Franco Modigliani of M.I.T. — revised their models so as to incorporate values representing inflationary expectations. It turned out that their models tracked capital spending far more accurately than before. In addition, Alan Greenspan has suggested that since the mid-1960's companies have been revising upward their forecasts of future rates of wage inflation. Rising rates of inflation encourage businessmen to replace old equipment faster.

Businessmen tend to deny that they invest in capital goods in order to beat inflation. Two years ago, a *Fortune* survey of executives in manufacturing found most of them insisting that they were maintaining their heavy spending for other reasons — e.g., simply because it was required to meet long-term demand. The question has by no means been resolved; still, those "other reasons" seem to have been less compelling in less inflationary periods. The view that inflation powerfully affects capital-investment decisions was bolstered by the sequence of events in 1968–69, when inflation was strong and when the level of appropriations remained high — even though utilization of existing plant and equipment in manufacturing had declined markedly. It had reached a cyclical high of 91 percent in 1966, but averaged only 84 percent in 1969, a level at which economists are not used to witnessing substantial increases in appropriations. The cutbacks did not begin this time until the end of 1969, when the utilization rate was approaching 80 percent. (It is now estimated to be around 75 percent, and appropriations have recently been 20 percent below the 1969 peak.)

Inflation seems to have affected the composition as well as the total of capital spending. There has been a continuing shift in recent years in the shares of spending going for plant and for equipment. The totals spent on equipment — machinery, vehicles, and fixtures — expanded nearly three times as fast in the 1960's as did spending on plants and structures. In the latter half of the decade, spending on plant declined to 29 percent of total capital outlays, down from an average of 36 percent during 1947–64 (and more than 50 percent in 1929). In part this shift in the composition of spending reflects the fact that some of the depreciation reforms of the 1960's applied only to machinery or did not encourage purchases of structures. In part the shift may also reflect the fact that equipment has grown complex and sophisticated more rapidly than structures have. An automated warehouse, for example, entails relatively higher outlays for machinery than did the contents of an old-fashioned warehouse in which goods were handled manually. But another large reason for the shift was the massive inflation in construction costs during the 1960's. The inflation, in effect, gave businessmen a considerable incentive to avoid building new plants if they possibly could, and to use existing floor space and structures more efficiently.

Taking everything together, it seems likely that inflation has some long-term tendency to raise the capital-output ratio. And so if, as is widely believed, the U.S. has slid into an era of permanent inflation, then there are apt to be permanent pressures to raise the capital-spending totals.

Less for manufacturing

Although it is impossible to be precise about the size of private capital spending toward the end of this decade, it seems possible to suggest which sectors of the economy will generate the spending and which will be weak. The share of manufacturing, which accounted for 40 percent of all capital outlays made by industry last year, is apt to decline by a couple of percentage points. In part this prospective decline is related to some highly visible problems of particular manufacturing industries; in part it is related to the extraordinary growth prospects of some other industries.

One problem area in manufacturing is the steel industry, where profits have been weak and where, even if profits recover, spending may be concentrated in cheaper technologies in the future — electric furnaces, for example — than it has been in the past. The textile and shoe industries, which are heavily beset by foreign competition and asking for protection, are also obvious problem areas.

In several other manufacturing industries the prospects for spending must be classified as uncertain. The food and beverage industries may come up with new products that require a great deal of capital spending (as freeze-dried coffee did several years ago), but at the same time other facilities might become redundant. An economist and specialist in the food industry, Gordon F. Bloom of M.I.T., believes that a lot of capital can be eliminated in, for example, the soft-drink business. Under present arrangements one company typically makes the concentrate, another mixes it with water and bottles the product. The bottles may then be shipped in and out of warehouses before they get to the retailer and, finally, the consumer. Savings could be made all around, Bloom suggests, if the consumer had equipment for mixing the concentrate and water himself — an arrangement some manufacturers are already thinking of.

Future expenditures by the petroleum industry are also somewhat problematical. They will be heavily influenced by what happens to U.S. oil properties abroad, by the future of import quotas, and possibly by new antipollution regulations concerning the use of fuel oil and gasoline. Pollution and safety regulations also make the level of spending by the auto industry an uncertain proposition. A *Fortune* estimate of the capital-investment prospects of different industries shows weak or doubtful prospects for the manufacturers that all together accounted for 45 percent of capital outlays by manufacturers last year.

Waiting for some booms

Investment prospects for some manufacturers seem strong, however. The expected boom in housing and government construction will presumably generate a fair amount of spending by the housing and building-material companies. Rubber companies should also be large spenders: they are the principal manufacturers of the polymeric materials and products that are increasingly apt to replace wood and metals. The instrument companies, which, among other things, manufacture measuring and sensing devices to detect pollution and control automated machinery, will be called on to spend a lot more. Laser manufacturers may have to supply a growing number of devices for such purposes as cutting, increasing the precision of machinery, holography, possibly projecting television images. Sales of lasers and associated equipment may rise from some $300 million now to $1 billion in ten years.

Manufacturers of computers and nonelectric machinery will have to increase their spending a great deal as there is increased use of numerically controlled machine tools and robot devices. Most of the computer makers' capital outlays, of course, are for machines they keep on their own balance sheets and lease to others. The industry's past rate of growth in shipments, something over 20 percent a year, will probably fall below the 20 percent level in the near future. A fair amount of its domestic market penetration has already taken place, and major changes in the central processing units will probably come along more slowly than before. However, the addition or substitution of modular parts in computers will increase. Strong growth is also expected in mini-computers and peripheral equipment. One especially interesting growth prospect involves the sales of computer terminals to banks, stock brokerage houses, and retailers; all of them will be searching for ways to substitute computer processes for the blizzard of paper now deluging them.

Another group that will probably have to expand capacity considerably over the decade is the electrical-machinery industry. Its major products are turbines and generators, as well as power transmission and distribution equipment, and it goes without saying that the electric-utility industry will need a lot of these products to eliminate present shortages and service deficiencies and to meet future demands.

Outside manufacturing there are several areas whose growth prospects are fairly obvious. The list begins with the communication companies. A.T. & T. wants to improve service, of course, and is also estimating that its telephone traffic will more than double by 1980 — and that its revenues from data transmission will grow ninefold. The needs of the public utilities are also fairly obvious. Utilities and communication companies together accounted for nearly 30 percent of 1970's capital outlays.

Moving the people

Among the large uncertainties about the capital-goods markets are several having to do with government policy. One question concerns population distribution. A great deal of attention is now being paid in Washington to the proposition that future population growth should be redirected — that some of it should be channeled into new communities and that some measures might be taken to redistribute some of the present population. David Rockefeller has suggested that initial capital of at least $10 billion would be required to build the new communities needed in the U.S. in the years ahead. (One frequently published estimate is that the U.S. will need 110 of these communities by the year 2000.) The Department of Housing and Urban Development has already begun to assist in the development of a few such communities.

The consequences for capital spending of any such policies could be momentous. Any policy to build new population centers might require much larger capital expenditures — e.g., for shopping centers, office buildings, factories, communication facilities, hospitals, and churches — than would a policy of simply letting existing centers grow. Glenn Seaborg, the former chairman of the Atomic Energy Commission, has suggested that the huge nuclear power stations to be built in the years ahead might become the centers of what he calls "Nuplexes" — major industrial areas that would be located near new cities.

Another large uncertainty about the capital-goods markets concerns the availability of financing. Many people in the financial community are concerned that there will not be enough funds to underwrite large investments by business, by municipalities, and by the federal government (e.g., for transportation and housing programs). They fear that the demand for financing will press so hard against supply that interest rates will rise to still new heights, thereby curtailing plans for a good many projects. However, limited supply may not be the real problem: the more significant issue may turn out to be whether private industry will be able to service all the additional debt that current projections suggest it will have to take on. It is not clear that corporations will be able to find enough lenders for the types of borrowing they will need and also not clear that they will be able to keep their interest burdens at a manageable level by raising substantial amounts of capital in the equity markets. A.T.& T.'s financial position furnishes a current example of the debt-service problem. Its ratio of debt to total capital has jumped to 46 percent, versus only 31½ percent as recently as 1965. Chairman H. I. Romnes said at the 1971 annual meeting, "We are rapidly closing in on the limit of debt a business like ours can prudently carry."

A final cluster of uncertainties about the capital-goods markets concerns the new role of foreigners in the markets. Rising purchases of foreign equipment are assuming major importance in the capital-spending picture. Imports are clearly gaining on home-produced items. It is true that sales of domestically made capital goods have increased in absolute amounts during the last decade; buying of domestic equipment was $29 billion greater than that of foreign-made equipment in 1960, and the gap rose to $57 billion by 1970. But the share of imported goods meanwhile mounted from 2 percent to 8 percent, as imports rose from $600 million to $5 billion. A continuation of this more rapid growth rate would eventually result in a narrowing of the absolute gap and in tremendous foreign inroads on the sales of domestic equipment producers.

In addition, it is important to note that the foreign affiliates of U.S. companies are increasing their capital spending far more rapidly abroad than are companies in the U.S. Spending abroad was up 22 percent in 1970 and was projected to rise 16 percent in 1971, while spending in the U.S. has been stagnating. If such disparities continue, they may someday cause present projections of capital spending in the U.S. to look very optimistic indeed.

The sum of all the numerous uncertainties is a large new question about the future trend of the capital-output ratio. The recent rise in the ratio may turn out, in retrospect, to have represented no more than the effects of a rather special cyclical boom. But it may also turn out to have been the beginning of a quite new economic era — one in which more capital is needed to produce a given quantity of goods. We will doubtless not get a definite answer to the question for some time. Meanwhile, the fact that there is a question is itself a major economic event.

Seven

The Mounting Bill
for Pollution Control

Some of the biggest investment decisions of the decade will
concern capital goods that protect the air and water but may
have no dollar payoff at all.

Amid the crazy-quilt jumble of multicolored pipes, tanks, and other structures at the giant Dow Chemical facility at Midland, Michigan, a microcosm of U.S. industry's spiraling investment in pollution control is in the making. Under construction or in the planning stages are twenty-eight cooling towers that will together cost more than $7 million. A $1,500,000 incinerator, first of its kind in the world, will burn waste tars cleanly. Hundreds of thousands of dollars are going into dikes that ring storage tanks. A motorized patrol prowls around the plant, its instruments sniffing out any chemicals that might have escaped into the air. Technicians recently surveyed all the 4,522 vents in the Midland facility and are in the process of curtailing odor emissions at every one where there is a problem.

Dow is also working hard to protect the Tittabawassee River, which flows lazily through the middle of the company's property. Over the years the river has been of great importance to Midland, serving as a heat sink and carrier of discarded wastes. Now, says general manager Harold Bosscher, "our goal is to get out of that river." The company has spent almost $1 million on a water-diversion system that should prevent the accidental discharge of effluents into the river. One portent of the future is a new chlor-alkali production facility that is entirely self-contained — it has no outfalls to the river. In addition, the cooling towers will cut in half the heat load that earlier went into the Tittabawassee. And by recycling the water, the towers will also reduce by 45 percent, or 100 million gallons, the plant's daily intake of water *from* the river.

All together, some $8,500,000, which is 23 percent of 1971's capital spending at Midland, is going into efforts to control air and water pollution. Company-wide, such efforts will come to about $25 million in 1971. Much more will be spent in the years to come, with no end in sight. Says Bosscher: "I think it's a way of life."

Dow's campaign against pollution seems especially strenuous but certainly isn't unique these days. Capital spending for pollution control is rapidly emerging as an integral part of U.S. industrial operations. In 1971 U.S. manufacturing plants and utilities are believed to be spending at least $1.5 billion on air- and water-pollution control. This spending will accelerate, and the cumulative total for the next five years is apt to be close to $20 billion. These figures are estimates, based on projections that have been made by various industry groups and by the federal Environmental Protection Agency (EPA). They are, at best, approximations. There are vast discrepancies between the figures put forth by the pollution controllers and the estimates made by those subject to controls. For example, one recent EPA study put the cost of suppressing sulphur oxides from copper smelters at $87 million. The copper industry says that much larger outlays will be required — $345 million if new control technology works out, $1.2 billion if it doesn't (because the failure would require replacement of present smelters). In addition to being rough, the estimates on pollution-control outlays are necessarily incomplete; that $20-billion total excludes spending by government and by the transportation, service, and agricultural sectors of the economy. And note that the total refers only to spending associated with cleaner air and water; it excludes spending designed to deal with other kinds of environmental concerns — e.g., to suppress "noise pollution" and to dispose of solid waste.

A change in the rules of business

But while the dollar totals are most uncertain, there is no doubt at all that these outlays represent an epochal event for U.S. business. The new laws and other pressures on businessmen, requiring vast investments on which (more often than not) there can be no direct return, represent a fundamental alteration of "the rules" of business. The alteration has been noted by the new Chairman of the Securities and Exchange Commission, William J. Casey, who announced in a recent speech that the commission may require companies filing financial statements with it to disclose the extent to which pollution-control spending might "materially affect the capital needs or earning power of the business." At many companies, the immediate consequence of the new rules will be a sacrificing of modernization and expansion plans in order to build facilities and buy equipment required for pollution control. Financially stronger corporations may be able to raise the funds to do both, straining the already pressured capital markets in the process. In either case, the productivity of capital will be adversely affected. Some economists have cited the need for further spending on pollution-control equipment as one reason why the capital-output ratio — which measures the amount of plant and equipment needed per unit of output — may rise in the years ahead, after declining for many years.

The previous chapters have identified this country's new concerns with the environment, and with the quality of life generally, as a major source of uncertainty about the economy in the years ahead. Conceivably, these concerns might lead to renunciation of economic growth as a national goal. But even if there is no formal renunciation of growth, it seems clear that those outlays to improve the environment will in fact work to hold down growth. In that sense, pollution control is an island of certainty in a sea of uncertainties.

The cost of sulphur oxides

The biggest spenders on pollution control today are industries that are often described as being the biggest polluters: utilities, steel, oil, paper, chemicals. But many of their problems, particularly those associated with the combustion of fuel, are actually shared by a lot of industries. A lot of them, it seems clear, will be spending heavily in efforts to control sulphur and nitrogen oxides.

Sulphur oxides are probably the most pervasive of all air contaminants, and they present an unparalleled challenge to designers of pollution-control systems. Smelters, refineries, and many other industrial plants contribute a significant share of the SO_2 spewed into the air, but more than half of it — an astounding 20 million tons a year — is generated by coal- and oil-burning power plants. According to estimates by the EPA, sulphur oxides cause damage to health, materials, property, and vegetation that amounts to $8.3 billion a year. That works out to about 10 cents in damage for each pound of sulphur oxides now emitted into the atmosphere.

Unless it is brought under control, the emission of sulphur oxides will nearly quadruple by the end of this century, to an estimated annual total of 125 million tons. Even though nuclear power plants, which generate no air pollution, are expected to be supplying more than 50 percent of this country's electricity by the year 2000, up dramatically from less than 2 percent today, the total output of electricity is expected to rise six or seven times above today's level. Which would leave us burning about three times the amount of fossil fuels consumed today — and generating more sulphur oxides.

Right now there is no economically viable technology that can effectively suppress sulphur oxide emissions. Scrubbing the oxides with limestone and trapping sulphuric acid mist in the stack are two methods now under investigation. But these and some of the other methods create new pollution and waste-disposal problems. For instance, mountains of calcium sulphate are generated in the limestone process; there is no market for it, and it can become a water pollutant. At an 800-megawatt coalfired power plant, a limestone scrubbing system may cost $15 million to install. Some of the other control techniques, which can be twice as expensive, convert sulphur dioxide into sulphuric acid or elemental sulphur. But that is no panacea either. The sulphuric acid produced in this manner is often of poor quality, is difficult to store, and is hard to market. Right now, furthermore, elemental sulphur recovered from SO_2 isn't exactly something the U.S. economy is waiting for with bated breath — there are vast quantities of it already on the market and prices have been declining for some years. Any large-scale production of sulphur at pollution-control installations would only worsen the glut.

A tax that purifies

The most effective method of reducing emissions of sulphur oxides so far has been to shift to low-sulphur fuel — supplies of which are limited. Standard Oil (New Jersey), for one, has poured $200 million into construction of desulphurizing facilities in the Caribbean and expects to spend a lot more money in similar efforts to increase the supply. Persistent pressures by government authorities to reduce sulphur content will force more capital spending on desulphurizing plants. A new code in New York City, for instance, is expected to limit sulphur in fuel to 0.3 percent by the end of this year. Much of the fuel burned in New York today has a 1 percent sulphur content.

To speed up sulphur oxide control technology, President Nixon has proposed a tax on sulphur in fuel. The tax in one version being considered would be paid by oil and coal companies. (There is no technology available to remove sulphur from coal.) They would pass it on in the form of higher fuel costs to utilities and other fuel users; and the users would get a tax rebate from the government, the size of the rebate depending on the sulphur content of the emission. The federal government would apply the tax funds to the development of control technology and also to develop new supplies of clean energy.

But even the cleanest fuels will leave their users with some large new capital-spending problems. Natural gas, for example, which is ordinarily sulphur-free, generates other kinds of pollutants and demands substantial new capital outlays for modifications of existing boilers and other equipment. Natural low-sulphur oil now in use often contains more paraffin than the high-sulphur variety. It solidifies unless the lines through which it runs are heated to a fairly high temperature. Although precise industry-wide figures are lacking, the cost to utilities of insulating fuel lines and making other modifications to handle low-sulphur oil will probably come to hundreds of millions of dollars. Pacific Gas & Electric Co. alone is spending more than $2 million on these modifications and New York's Con Edison has spent $4 million.

A somewhat similar problem is created by the use of low-sulphur coal. Perversely, the older fly-ash-catching electrostatic precipitators work better on high-sulphur than low-sulphur coal. Most existing precipitator installations, therefore, must be enlarged and modified. Alternatively, some other types of cleaning devices, such as wet scrubbers or baghouses, might be bought, at a cost of millions of dollars.

Pollutants from the clean fuels

Unfortunately, neither low-sulphur fuels nor devices to scrub sulphur dioxide do much to reduce emissions of another dangerous pollutant, nitrogen oxides, which with hydrocarbons are the main contributors to photochemical smog. Nitrogen oxides are created by high-temperature combustion, and they may appear in quantity even if natural gas is used. Their control requires an entirely different technology — one that is still largely undeveloped and that might end up costing the utilities something like $1.7 billion in capital outlays in the next five years to control emissions from existing boilers.

A pioneering effort to slash nitrogen oxide emissions is in progress at P. G. & E. It began when the company, which burns no coal but only natural gas and low-sulphur oil, nevertheless found itself in trouble when it added a big new generating unit to its plant at Moss Landing, California, in 1968. A brownish-yellow cloud began to form downwind from the plant. Tests revealed much higher levels of nitrogen oxides than either P. G. & E. or the boiler manufacturer had anticipated. Ever since, P. G. & E. has been trying in a variety of ways to modify the gas burners at Moss Landing.

First, the company has cut the amount of excess air in the

burners and resorted to two-stage combustion. This has slashed nitrogen oxide emissions from a high of 1,500 parts per million to about 140 to 150 p.p.m. P. G. & E. isn't stopping there, but is working to reduce emissions still further through gas recirculation. The big bad clouds are gone now; yet the air is still sometimes discolored on days when there is a temperature inversion in the Moss Landing area. (Automobile traffic is believed to contribute to these smogs.) All together, the cost of suppressing nitrogen oxides on that one generating unit alone will amount to $600,000. If it's fully successful, the system will be installed, at a cost of several million, throughout P. G. & E.'s far-flung service territory in California.

But even if P. G. & E.'s system works, the problem of nitrogen oxides will be only partly solved. Two-stage combustion and gas recirculation are applicable to gas- and oil-fueled boilers but hard to use with coal boilers, which account for nearly half of U.S. utilities' total generating capacity. In fact, two-stage combustion may *never* be used on coal boilers because of the danger of explosion. Gas recirculation in coal boilers also involves some such danger, and besides it appears to reduce nitrogen oxide emissions from the boilers only slightly.

The solution is nuclear

Of the industries that will be spending heavily on pollution control in the 1970's, the utilities — which now account for about 15 percent of all private capital spending — would appear to face the greatest challenges. They discharge massive quantities of sulphur and nitrogen oxides and other pollutants into the air, and massive quantities of warm water into lakes and rivers.

The technological problems of pollution control have been solved by the industry, but politics and economics keep getting in its way. The technological solution to the problem of those air pollutants is nuclear power. No dirty air swirls around atomic plants; they don't emit any. To be sure, they disgorge vast amounts of heated water — up to 70 percent more than steam-electric plants. But there are technologies to deal with this too. Instead of taking water from a nearby stream or lake and then returning the warmed-up water to its source after it has cooled the plant's steam condensers, utilities can discharge it into artificial ponds and canals. Or, since water for cooling purposes is becoming scarce inland, they might make major efforts to gain access to the oceans. But very little ocean-front industrial property is available these days. (One reason it is unavailable, especially in California, is that environmentalists have fought utilities' efforts to get such property.) Charles F. Luce, chairman of Con Ed, said recently that by the end of this decade his company might be placing new generating plants on man-made islands in the Atlantic, about ten miles offshore.

But for many utilities the answer is likely to be cooling towers, and these are in fact sprouting all over the country. Conservationists recently forced utilities with plants on Lake Michigan to start installing them; some environmentalists have even talked about equipping oceanside plants with cooling towers. The only difficulty is economic. It costs about $1,700,000 to install a mechanical-draft tower at an average power plant and more than $4 million to install a natural-draft tower (which is larger but less expensive to operate). All told, U.S. utilities and industrial plants are expected to install about $2 billion worth of towers and other cooling facilities during the next five years.

Meanwhile there are persistent political and economic difficulties about clean nuclear-generated electricity. The environmentalists have resurrected the issue of nuclear safety in the last couple of years, thereby doing a lot to delay progress toward cleaner air. Regulatory procedures have also worked against nuclear power. It takes engineers years to design the hardware needed for a nuclear plant. And after it is designed, companies may have to wait as long as seven years before regulators approve it. P. G. & E.'s president, Shermer L. Sibley, regards any such delays as potentially disastrous. The hardware could become obsolete before it was built, and conservationists might come up with reasons that could not have been foreseen to block construction. Says Sibley: "There must be a better way to do it, both environmentally and economically."

The eardrum-shattering drama of steelmaking generates pollutants by the ton — but, more and more, the dust, smoke, and dirty water are being stopped at the source. Despite its recent poor profitability and low return on investment, the steel industry has emerged as a big spender on pollution control. Since 1951, according to the American Iron and Steel Institute, it has invested more than $1 billion on controls. Further pollution-related capital spending, amounting to perhaps $2 billion, is in prospect for the next five years. (Right now the industry is spending more than $1.5 billion a year for all capital goods.)

These expenses will hit steel hard. Consider, for example, their impact at Bethlehem Steel. In the past twenty years, Bethlehem has spent $200 million on pollution control at its plants, works, mines, quarries, and shipyards; it expects to spend $250 million more in the next five years. Financial Vice President James H. Walker observes that these outlays hurt in two ways. First, they represent a diversion of funds that might have earned a direct return. Second, this capital spending entails additional *operating* costs — typically 10 percent of the original outlays. Air-pollution control devices, such as electrostatic precipitators and scrubbers, are notoriously undependable and require frequent maintenance and attention. One operating man at Bethlehem suggests that in general it costs twice as much to maintain pollution-control equipment as it does to maintain steelmaking tools. Walker figures that all together his company's pollution-control costs will reduce net income by $90 million during the next five years. "Our best estimate is that, if we continue on this basis, it will cost us over $1 a share in the fifth year."

The cost of crowding

The costs soar when the basic steelmaking facility is an old one. Bethlehem operates one of the country's oldest steelmaking facilities at Lackawanna, New York, a suburb of Buffalo. At the crowded Lackawanna plant, where mules once supplied propulsive power for coal wagons, engineers have been forced to go straight up into the air in designing new control facilities. They had to reinforce with steel and concrete the roofs of old structures so that they could safely put air-pollution control devices atop them. Similarly, lack of space at Lackawanna demanded construction of huge cylindrical filtering tanks, spread around different parts of the plant, in which process water is now filtered to crystal clarity before it is released back into Lake Erie. At Burns Harbor, where low-slung buildings stretch over 3,300 acres of land, Bethlehem engineers were able to build a central treatment facility to serve the entire plant.

In the steel industry, as in quite a few others, the new technologies generally present fewer pollution problems than the older ones. The gradual closing of open-hearth furnaces and their replacement by the more efficient and cleaner basic-oxygen furnaces have somewhat reduced the dimensions of the pollution-control task. Increased use of direct-reduction techniques, in which ore is reduced to iron with no need for coke ovens and blast furnaces, will also help. Much further in the future we may even see the emergence of direct chemical reduction of ore to steel; that might eliminate air pollution from steelmaking entirely.

The oil industry is one of many facing huge uncertainties about the size of future spending on pollution control. The oil industry has a "pollution potential" that is probably unmatched; its basic product can damage both air and water, and there are possibilities of damage in drilling, refining, and transportation. Procedures for avoiding oil spillage in the oceans, and the cost of implementing them, are now under international consideration. Traffic-direction systems, as elaborate as air-traffic control, for the world's large ocean-going tankers may be worked out for particularly busy ports. Standard Oil Co. (New Jersey) is testing improved navigational aids that cost $200,000 per tanker. Under consideration is a worldwide system of portside facilities at which tankers could pump their dirty ballast for treatment; these would cost a total of perhaps $1.6 billion.

In the U.S., according to the American Petroleum Institute, the oil industry has spent $1.2 billion in the past five years on capital equipment to clean dirty air and water. Spending is apt to soar because of the pace at which new pollution-control regulations have been evolving. Right now the industry seems likely to be confronted with a demand for substantial capital spending to reduce gasoline-vapor emissions at filling stations. And it will have to spend vast sums on refinery equipment designed to produce low-lead gasoline.

In some industries the new environmental concerns are coming at a fairly opportune time. In paper manufacturing, the pressures to clean up coincide to a considerable extent with a need to replace old plants that would soon be obsolescent anyway. The paper industry will be spending about $200 million a year on capital equipment related to cleaner water and air in the next few years.

Probably in the best position of all is the chemical industry, where significant control of pollution can be achieved through process changes that transform byproduct streams into new sources of raw materials. Says Bosscher of Dow: "From an operating man's standpoint, the emphasis on waste control is one of the better things that has happened to us. It sharpened up our whole operation. We will not accept a plant today that doesn't have its pollution control in hand before it's built." And, Bosscher adds, pollution-control measures at Midland reduced raw-material leakages and losses and made possible a yield improvement worth about $6 million in the past three years.

The economics of two deadlines

Capital spending on pollution control is apt to be especially heavy in the next few years, as business rushes to comply with two important deadlines recently set by the Environmental Protection Agency. One requires the states to implement tough new national air-quality standards by the middle of 1975. The standards call for significant reduction in emissions of sulphur oxides, particulates (soot and smoke), carbon monoxide, hydrocarbons, nitrogen oxides, and photochemical oxidants. While some of the standards are far ahead of the control technology — they are far ahead in the case of sulphur and nitrogen oxides — they should at least introduce nationwide uniformity into the control measures.

The other deadline is for a permit system that will begin to take effect later this year, whose effect will be to penalize some 40,000 industrial plants in proportion to the amounts of effluents they discharge into streams and lakes. Aside from outlays for installations to reduce those effluents, the system will require the companies to invest heavily in measuring instruments. William D. Ruckelshaus, the energetic administrator of the EPA, calls it "a much more equitable system" because it will tend to equalize the economic impact of controls on competing companies located in different parts of the country.

But it is clear that, over all, the impact on profits will be extremely variable. It will vary, not only with the technologies involved but with the ability of industries to pass on the costs. Many small companies and branch operations of large ones have already shut down because of their owners' inability to meet the costs of pollution control, and more such shutdowns are in store. One recent EPA survey turned up ninety-two plants and other facilities in a wide variety of industries that have been forced to close down because of these costs. Indeed, the federal government has made it clear that it is reconciled to the possibility that some industries won't be able to live with the new regulations. It was Congress, fed up with years of foot dragging by some industries, that deleted references to "economic feasibility" from the new legislation. Ruckelshaus puts it this way: "In the Clean Air Act I'm mandated by Congress to set a standard that will protect public health. It doesn't say protect public health if we can afford it or if the costs are not exorbitant — it says protect public health. So to that extent there is built into the law the factor of ignoring the cost."

Actually, the EPA has already identified some of the industries it expects to be in trouble because of the regulations. In "The

Economics of Clean Air," the agency's report to Congress in March 1971, the gray-iron-foundry industry is named one of those "most severely affected by air pollution control." Says the report: "The nonuniformity of control regulations and costs, along with the lack of investment capital, will force most foundries to postpone implementation of control for as long as possible. Many firms, faced with reduced profit margins and an inability to raise capital for pollution control will be forced to merge or go out of business."

The report analyzed a total of seventeen industries and concluded that their cases varied considerably. Seven of them would "be able to raise their prices, thus passing the cost of control to the consumer." The seven: asphalt batching, coal cleaning, elemental phosphorus, phosphate fertilizer, grain milling and handling, iron and steel, and kraft pulp. The study suggested that three industries — petroleum refining, petroleum storage, and rubber (tire manufacture) — would "recover valuable materials in sufficient quantities to offset all of the annual cost of control." That left the gray-iron foundries and six other industries that would "probably absorb part of the cost of control, reducing their revenues from sales, taxes paid, and net profits." These were cement, primary and secondary nonferrous metallurgy, varnish, brick and tile, and lime.

The savings are imagined

Fortune's interviews with executives in many different industries show them in general to be much less sanguine than the federal government about this ability to pass on or offset the cost of controls. Raymond W. Winkler, environmental conservation coordinator for Standard Oil, was typical in his skepticism. Referring to the government's assertion that in oil refining and storage the cost of recovered materials would *fully* offset the costs of controlling air pollution, Winkler said, "It would take a real stretch of the imagination to support that conclusion."

Several conclusions would seem to follow from the fact of

these substantial new pressures on profits. One is that business must explore all possible economies associated with pollution control. There is, for example, "cross-cycling" between plants, so that hot or cold water, or waste materials, can be profitably exchanged — thus reducing the need to build control facilities. In addition, far too little attention has been paid to regional waste-treatment plants, at which companies and municipalities might band together to achieve a saving on both capital and operating expenses. One big push in that direction might come soon if Du Pont and other companies on the lower Delaware River join the Deepwater Regional Sewerage System being developed by the Delaware River Basin Commission with the technical assistance of Engineering-Science, Inc., an affiliate of Zurn Industries. This ambitious enterprise, which already has a pilot plant operating at Du Pont's Chambers Works, envisions one central processing plant linked by pipelines to at least a dozen large industrial plants and small municipalities in the area.

A *need for clear standards*

It would also seem to follow that business, while cooperating with government regulators, must demand that standards be clarified before investments have to be made. At its Seattle plant about ten years ago, Bethlehem paid $400,000 for a baghouse that captures 90 percent of the fumes from two furnaces. But to meet today's higher standards, the company will have to invest $2,400,000 in another baghouse to collect the remaining 10 percent of the dirt. If Bethlehem had got the regulations all at once, instead of in stages, its total investment could have been substantially lower.

There may be a large problem about one of the standards recently called for by the Environmental Protection Agency. A recent study suggests that the proposed nationwide standard of 100 micrograms per cubic meter for nitrogen oxides could prove to be either too stringent or too lenient; we still have a lot to learn about the effects of nitrogen oxides. The authors of the study, Simon K. Mencher, former deputy commissioner of the New York City Department of Air Resources, and Howard M. Ellis, a professor at City University of New York, urged the EPA not to require massive capital spending for nitrogen oxide control until both health standards and control techniques are better developed. There is no doubt that a lot of money spent on industrial pollution control has already been wasted because of constantly changing regulations. Sibley of P. G. & E. fears that a lot more will be lost because of government decisions "made on an emotionally enforced basis."

There is some evidence that emotionalism about the deterioration of the environment is beginning to give way to a more hard-headed concern, in which the economic realities of fighting pollution are taken into account. Hendrik S. Houthakker, at the time a member of the Council of Economic Advisers (he has since resigned to return to teaching), attracted a great deal of attention in April 1971 with a speech arguing that we must pay more heed to the "social cost" of environmental controls — and that these might be too large in some cases to justify proposed controls. The Environmental Protection Agency has only recently established an economic unit that is looking into industry's pollution-control costs.

But there are still tremendous gaps in our knowledge of what pollution-control measures will cost and what they will accomplish. Says Walter Hamilton, executive director of the National Industrial Pollution Control Council: "I can't remember any other situation in which we have moved out on something that had so massive an economic and social impact with so inadequate a data base."

Eight

"A New Nation"
Gropes for Better Government

The U.S. can't have a healthy economy unless it improves
the quality of its politics. One key question: How can
decision-making processes be modified to reflect the greater
freedom and diversity of the people?

The U.S. entered the Seventies with its economy in a relatively mild recession and its political life in a profound and frightening depression. For most of the last fifty years the ups and downs of the economy have provided the main theme of the great American suspense story. In the decade ahead the business system will confront an extraordinarily high level of uncertainty. Nevertheless, anxieties (and hopes) during the Seventies will turn more on the quality of government — federal, state, and local — than on the vigor of the economy itself. The main hazards facing the economy are, in fact, governmental.

These include such specific and familiar uncertainties as Washington's skill in controlling inflation and reducing the swings of the business cycle. They also include the impact of taxes and of government regulation. Total taxes as a percentage of gross national product may increase during the Seventies, although the increase probably will not be large. There will almost surely be a lot more regulation, especially in the areas of consumer and environmental protection.

As to both taxes and regulation, the crucial uncertainties lie in the quality, the wisdom, of particular government policies. Taxes are not merely high or low; there can be wise and unwise taxes, fair and unfair taxes. In regulation the range of quality is even wider. For instance, many businessmen admit, in principle, the need for more governmental protection of the environment; but they are understandably appalled at the possibility that the quality of the regulation will be as clumsily destructive as, say, federal regulation of railroads has been.

Aside from all such specific governmental interventions, there is one important respect in which the health of the economy depends on the quality of political life. The condition of business is affected by the basic self-confidence, the morale, of the society as a whole. One of the essential elements of a society's morale is trust in government — and the public's opinion of government in the U.S. has seldom if ever been as low as it is now.

This discontent is not a partisan matter. It is shared by members of both major parties and by the increasing proportion who attach themselves to no party. It is shared even by many of those in public office. President Nixon was not contradicted by his fellow politicians (or by voters) when in his 1971 State of the Union message he said: "Let's face it. Most Americans today are simply fed up with government at all levels." That is indeed the most important and uncontroverted single fact about the condition of the U.S. today.

It's true, of course, that the American attitude toward government has seldom been characterized by enthusiasm or even docility. But the present public mood is very different from the old skepticism and grumbling, and different from the waves of political disapproval summed up by the recurring slogan, "Turn the rascals out!" In the past, any general public criticism of governmental performance was usually accompanied by a rather clear picture of how it might be done better. One of the most disquieting aspects of the present scene is the absence of any strong, widely held vision of political alternatives.

Even today's lunatic fringes lack confidence in the practical application of their lunacies. A generation ago many highly educated Americans regarded the Soviet system as a superior alternative. A larger number hoped for the establishment here of democratic socialism. We even had some fascists, and they too knew what they wanted. These positive, if heretical, faiths have declined among us; instead we have self-styled Maoists and Guevarists whose political scenarios are almost entirely devoted to the techniques of disorganizing society. Today's revolutionaries display little or no interest in how the pieces might be reassembled into a better political system.

The economic disaster of the Thirties developed a clear-cut cleavage between those who applauded every expansion of governmental activity and those who revived an old — although never dominant — American belief that the best government was the least. Recently, as faith in bigger and bigger government has declined, the opposite camp has not waxed in influence. Public opinion became more politicized than ever in the Sixties, but the size of government was no longer the dominant issue. As a touchstone of political attitudes, the slogan "less government" now seems as obsolete as the slogan "more government."

The overriding challenge of the Seventies will not be how to expand or to reduce the size of government. The task will be the more difficult one of improving the quality of government so that it fits better with the evolving character of American society.

The higher meaning of the commerce clause

Though many Americans prefer to think of the U.S. in terms of material progress, the primacy of politics over economics is deeply embedded in the logic of the nation's development. The U.S. represented a political breakthrough for a century before it became also a business marvel. Its later economic success was essentially a projection of the same faith in the cooperation of free individuals that had long characterized its political system. Economic failure, as the great depression demonstrated, could have far-reaching political consequences. But the fundamental dependence, as we are now painfully reminded, runs the other way: in the long pull, this country cannot be healthier than its politics.

Civilized men, especially in a democracy that is pluralist in religious and philosophical belief, look to government as the main symbol and test of their ability to live together. If they lose a basic trust in the legitimacy and efficacy of government, they will not find a substitute for it in economic prosperity. Indeed, they will not long preserve prosperity. Without faith in government, investment will dry up, credit will contract, consumers will restrict purchases. (Who wants to buy a house in an area with a grossly incompetent local government?)

The economic activity of individuals and groups makes sense and becomes fruitful only within some general arrangement, some framework of law, larger than the economy itself. Consider, for example, the effect on economic activity of the interstate-commerce clause of the Constitution. It came into being at a time when a new kind of people, the Americans, had been "brought forth" into nationhood, and it turned out to be a wonderful expression of the new political reality.

Most commentaries on the clause over the years dwell on how it increased federal power at the expense of the states. But its more important effect was to create the political preconditions that made possible a nationwide market structure. The number, size, and range of decisions made by entities (mostly individuals) other than the federal government were eventually to be multiplied many times because this market structure existed. Moreover, the total economic action became more lively, innovative, efficient, and varied as the scope of competition widened from a local to a national range. In short, a government power was exerted in a way that expanded nongovernmental decision making and improved its quality.

Nearly two hundred years later all levels of American government are groping — painfully — in an effort to achieve another tremendous political advance along the same line as that exemplified by the history of the commerce clause. Once again, the underlying truth is that a new kind of people has come into the world, for the Americans of the 1970's are at least as different from their immediate predecessors as were those of the 1770's. The rise of prosperity, education, and freedom has set up new requirements for appropriate political institutions within which this changing people can express their choices, shape their lives.

Paradoxes for the Seventies

We have been underestimating the gravity of the political challenge now confronting us. As it was in the American beginning, the quest is to resolve in politics a set of paradoxes: unity and diversity, social cohesion and individuality, order and freedom. By now, however, the American character and circumstances have developed along a line that greatly increases the tension within these pairs and the difficulty of reconciling them in politics.

• National unity, for instance, has been intensified by the integrating influence of the economy, the educational system, and the communication networks. Yet the opposite pole, diversity, has been equally intensified by the specialization of knowledge and careers, the availability of a wide range of life styles, and the divergence of opinions and values that is encouraged by education.

• Attitudes toward jobs and products — and also toward love, marriage, war, and religion — are now more influenced by individuality, less determined by the society as a whole. Yet the need for social cohesion grows with our increasing economic and psychological dependence on one another.

• The individual becomes less and less amenable to restraint or coercion by superior authority. Yet the need for order simultaneously increases because every part of the society has become more vulnerable to events in other parts.

We can get at the essentials of our political problem by seeing the U.S. as a nation whose citizens are diverging in their goals, values, and life styles. Each citizen has, as a result of technology, education, organization, and prosperity, more range of action. Each, pursuing his own personal and group goals, has more power to hurt others — wittingly or unwittingly. Since a primary function of government is to protect citizens from one another, this changing situation seems to call for "more" government. But this simple conclusion can be dangerously misleading. Neither the citizens nor the complex society in which they operate are as susceptible as they were in former times to direct control by government power. Therefore new ways have to be found of harmonizing interests without substituting the raw coercive power of government for the increasing freedom of the citizen.

Ulysses Grant for Saigon?

The political requirements of the "new nation" dwarf the political problems of the past. That is why it is a mistake to say, as many do, that the quality of government has deteriorated. Considered as a thing apart, government has been improving markedly. Officeholders as a group are better qualified and probably better motivated than they used to be. They are more sensitive to the will and the interests of the public. Citizens, in turn, are more willing to participate in the political process. Graft and gross inefficiency have almost certainly declined. The schools are better. The police are better. The military services are better. The public hospitals are better. Even the tax structure is better.

But each of these improving aspects of government has registered a *relative* decline when it is stacked up against the present circumstances, needs, and values of the society. We will not understand the political crisis of the Seventies unless we see that it is a crisis of success — and therefore much harder to resolve than a crisis of failure. We cannot repent and retrace our steps, restoring our political life to some previous point in our history. Yesterday's schools, yesterday's police, yesterday's army, yesterday's politicians may have served yesterday more successfully than their counterparts serve today. But in terms of today's political needs, the men and institutions of the past would be even less adequate than those we now have. How would Ulysses S. ("Unconditional Surrender") Grant look in Vietnam? How would Horace Mann do in a Harlem classroom? What could Alexander Hamilton contribute as a member of the Council of Economic Advisers?

In any case, the political problems of the 1970's are not going to be solved by some new breed of angelic politicians. U.S. political leadership will be supplied by men now in office and in opposition — or men very like them. Moreover, many of the political problems these men will be dealing with are already in sight. And while economic forecasts for the Seventies contain an unusual degree of uncertainty, we can estimate roughly the resources that will be available and the cost of most government activities.

The standard forecast for the decade assumes a growth rate of around 4.3 percent. This would result in a 1980 G.N.P. of $1.5 trillion in 1970 dollars. *Fortune* assumes that federal spending will remain at about 21 percent of G.N.P., which would bring spending to $313 billion by 1980. It assumes also that state and local expenditures, which took 10.9 percent of G.N.P. in 1970, will continue their recent relative rise, and will reach at least 12 percent, or $179 billion, by the end of the decade.

But such projections provide no more than a sort of quantitative framework; they do not of themselves get to the heart of the main questions about government in the Seventies. More important than the dollar aggregates at the disposal of governments are questions about what the people, through their governments, decide to do with the dollars (e.g., whether to put additional spending stress on education or on health care). And more important than these issues of substantive priorities are questions of how the decision-making processes themselves might be restructured to a better fit with "the new nation." How do we determine what the people, in all their new diversities and freedoms, really want? How are their conflicts to be resolved, their priorities worked out, and their lines of advance determined?

Against that background we can speculate on how these new "constitutional" questions will apply to some specific governmental trends of the Seventies. We can begin with one of the most controversial trends of all — that concerning U.S. defense spending.

Security in a turbulent age

If federal expenditures in 1980 total $313 billion, how much of that might go for defense? In 1970 defense spending was $80.3 billion — 41 percent of the federal budget or 8.2 percent of G.N.P. If those proportions prevail in 1980, the U.S. will be

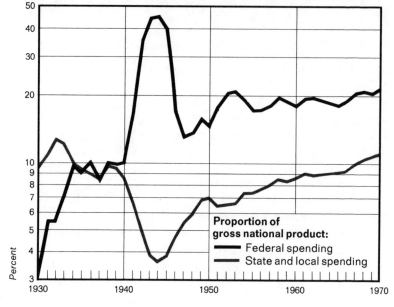

Some citizens who fear that power is being concentrated in Washington will be surprised by these charts. Federal government expenditure as a proportion of G.N.P. is where it was eighteen years ago. The chart below shows that federal civilian employees make up a substantially smaller proportion of the labor force than they did two decades ago. In both money and head count, the steep rise of the past two decades has been in state and local government — trends that are expected to continue through the Seventies.

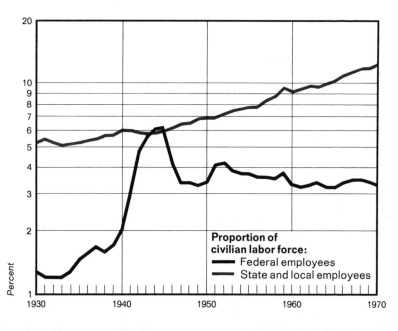

spending $123 billion on defense (at 1970 prices). Hardly any-
one believes the figure will be that high.

To get a closer look at the future of defense expenditures one
has to depart from simple arithmetic and observe some of the
trends, inside and outside the U.S., that will affect military
spending. Downward pressure will certainly be exerted by the
present wave of antimilitarism as an active, highly vocal force
within U.S. public opinion. Anxiety concerning the danger of
major Communist advances toward world domination is not now
as intense as it was in the Fifties and Sixties. Weak and new nations in Asia and Africa have not proved to be as vulnerable
to Communist pressures as Communist leaders expected —
and many Americans feared — they would be. The level of
nuclear power possessed by the U.S. and the U.S.S.R. "stabilizes"
relations between them in a horrible way (the balance of ter-
ror). There is solid hope that this tenuous stability can be translated into agreements on arms limitation.

Against these hopeful factors there is a formidable array of
conditions that may work to increase U.S. defense spending. The
world of the Seventies will almost certainly be turbulent, for reasons analogous to those that make order difficult to attain within
the U.S. Nations and groups within nations, conscious of their
divergent interests, have increased capabilities to pursue their
goals — which often conflict. Technology gives each of them
more power to harm others and more reason to fear others. Very
few people have great confidence that the existing structure of
world order (treaties, international law, the United Nations,
etc.) is strong enough to contain these new and turbulent forces.
The U.S. has accepted — and probably will continue to accept
— a substantial share of responsibility for buttressing and building the structure of world order. In the Seventies this will imply
the continued presence, if not the use, of a large and varied array of U.S. military force.

High-technology weaponry will continue to increase the cost
of armament per serviceman. Like almost all technology in the
twentieth century, military technology refuses to stand still (e.g.,
the current proposal for a new generation of nuclear subma-

rines). New developments, requiring huge new outlays, are forced on governments by the mere possibility of technological advances by competitor countries. This upward pressure on the U.S. defense budget will continue to be exerted, no doubt, through "the military industrial complex." But the real source of the pressure lies deeper — in the difficulty of freezing military technology.

Unit personnel costs will also advance as the U.S. tries to move closer to a volunteer army. The anticonscription sentiment behind this move is part of the very general American trend away from every kind of coercion, a trend that makes many government functions more difficult.

The U.S. and other advanced countries have recently been made aware of their vulnerability to violence by quite small groups. Even if world tensions diminish, even if arms-limitation agreements are highly successful, there will be so much armed freedom around, so many potentially violent wills in play, that U.S. defense costs will remain very high.

Considering all these elements, a rock-bottom defense budget might be $60 billion, or 4 percent of 1980's G.N.P. A much more likely figure is $90 billion, or 6 percent. Even the higher figure would reflect a substantial reordering of priorities — with defense expenditures dropping from 41 percent of 1970's federal budget to 29 percent in 1980.

The view from the bowling alley

The amount a nation spent on defense — and the industrial might that lay behind that figure — used to be a far better indicator of the nation's power than it is today. Victory now seems less and less inclined to perch on the banners of the side with the most battalions, the highest technology, or the biggest appropriations for armaments.

The effectiveness of U.S. military policy and foreign policy in the Seventies will depend on how wisely the nation interprets the bitter lessons of the Vietnam war. In some years the U.S. and its allies in Vietnam were probably spending at least thirty times as much as the North Vietnamese and their allies. Again and again, decision makers in Washington assumed during the Sixties that a further escalation of the U.S. effort must make the enemy quit. But all the expensive U.S. hardware, bought after shrewd and complex cost-benefit calculations, could not overcome certain nonquantifiable reactions in "the minds of men."

The enemy, refusing to recognize the "impossible" odds against him, went on fighting a low-technology, low-cost war. The South Vietnamese were too much detached from responsibility for what should have been *their* war by the size and technical sophistication of the U.S. intervention. The American people, as casualty rates rose, decided that the "cost-benefit ratio" of the war was unacceptable.

All these reactions suggest that in the Seventies the quality of U.S. foreign policy will depend more heavily on persuasion and less on raw military power than had been supposed at the beginning of the Sixties. Force to counter force will continue to be an indispensable ingredient of policy, but the rising importance of "the minds of men" — at home and abroad — will have to be reckoned more carefully in the equations of international action. Diplomacy, like domestic policy, has become a game with tens of millions of players. What is said and thought and felt in an Asian hamlet, a Paris bistro, a Detroit bowling alley, has become the prime business of the world's chancelleries — and not all the fearsome weaponry of the superpowers can outweigh that change.

Ironically, many of the severest critics of the Vietnam war have fallen into the same trap that caught the Pentagon and White House war planners. These critics, demanding that military spending be transferred to schools, health care, and urban problems, tend to assume that the level of funding will determine the results achieved in such domestic programs. It won't — for the same reason, basically, that U.S. expenditures were not decisive in Vietnam. In nearly all the domestic government functions that will be important in the Seventies, actual decision making will be very widely dispersed among millions of minds and wills that cannot be coerced or bought.

One familiar old type of government project relates primarily to *things.* Let us say that a government agency gets a congressional appropriation for a dam to generate electric power. The program's goal is clear and definite. The key questions, such as where on the river it should be sited and what kind of turbines should be installed, are all calculable. Tight control of the whole project can be maintained by the government agency.

How utterly different is such a government program as the war on poverty. There the agencies involved are not dealing with tons of inert matter or with highly predictable machines. The misnamed war on poverty is trying to reshape such impalpable and elusive objects as the attitudes, habits, perceptions, motivations, and goals of people.

For such a program huge sums of money are, no doubt, necessary. But the level of spending, as such, tells little or nothing about the results expectable. The jungle canopy that conceals stretches of the Ho Chi Minh Trail is transparent compared to the mists of doubt and controversy that hang over every policy question in the war on poverty.

Congress is now moving toward a version of President Nixon's Family Assistance Plan to replace the existing welfare system. The proposed substitute would further diminish direct government control of how the funds will actually be spent. A 1910-type poorhouse or orphan asylum exemplifies direct government management of the poor. The Family Assistance Plan is another step in a long, gradual shift to increased reliance on the decisions of the beneficiaries.

The effectiveness of any new welfare system will depend on the reaction to it of the poor and the nonpoor — individually and in groups. Because reactions, in the present state of knowledge, are very difficult to foresee, it is intrinsically far more difficult to design such a program than it is to put a (superbly trained, highly motivated) man on the moon by means of (predictable, pretested) machines.

There has been a fundamental shift in the character of federal payments generally; the recent trend of welfare payments is only part of the shift. Beginning in the Fifties, spending for direct federal purchases of goods and services has declined in relation to total federal spending. Meanwhile, there was a relative increase in funds for programs in which a substantial share of decision making was reserved for states, cities, universities, and individual citizens. Grants-in-aid, mostly to states and cities, made up 12 percent of the 1970 federal budget, and transfer payments to individuals (e.g., social-security payments) amounted to 30 percent.

Public discussion has not caught up with the significance of the new spending pattern. While some citizens deplore (and others cheer) "creeping socialism," meaning the centralizing of economic power in Washington, the fact is that a market-like kind of dispersed decision making has been gradually encroaching on the traditional style of government action by direct control. Washington now funnels an increasing share of the money it handles into nonfederal hands.

When the funnels are defective

The important qualitative questions now turn on how wisely government designs the funnels through which funds — and power — flow back into private hands. Bad funnels can influence private decision makers to employ the funds inefficiently or for socially undesirable ends. The Federal Housing Administration, while channeling billions of private funds into the housing market in the Forties and Fifties, had a hideous defect. Its refusal to guarantee mortgages in racially mixed neighborhoods strongly reinforced the preference of private decision makers for segregated housing.

Another example of a defective funnel is government activity in health care. For decades the American people have demonstrated, primarily through the market mechanism, that they were placing an ever higher priority on medical services. With medi-

care (for the aged) and medicaid (for those unable to pay for
medical services), government's presence in the health field has
been expanding.

If all we had to worry about was *how much* public money to
spend for health care, then public discussion of the priorities
could start with Senator Edward Kennedy's bill, which would
provide the largest outlays (around $70 billion) of all the pro-
posals now taken seriously. Citizens who did not place that high
a priority on health services could support some other bill with a
lower total figure — or oppose all such bills.

But we also have to face up to an entirely different set of con-
siderations, more important than the size of the tab. The market
for health services has been badly skewed by the combined
effect of commercial health insurance, medicare, medicaid, and
Blue Cross. Hospitalization is far better covered than care in
homes or doctors' offices. Preventive care is hardly covered at
all.

The significant day-to-day decisions in medical service are not
made by government officials, but by patients, physicians, and
hospital administrators. The present market structure is distorted
in such a way that the maximum pressure of demand falls on the
most expensive kind of service, hospitalization, for which prices
are rising very rapidly. Limited medical resources are inefficiently used when unnecessary decisions are made to hospitalize
the patient or keep him in hospitals longer. Few doctors consciously and cynically multiply hospital days for the purpose of
increasing their incomes. (For that matter, few relief recipients
consciously and cynically decide to stay on relief rolls rather
than develop work skills.) But a loaded decision structure exer-
cises a subliminal influence on all the private decision makers in
the health-services market.

The lag in education

This kind of market defect poses a novel range of problems for
government. Now it has to worry not only about the efficient

behavior of its own salaried servants, but about how the design of its money funnels will subtly affect the decisions and behavior of persons who are not under anyone's administrative control. Nowhere is this challenge more serious than in education.

The "new nation" that has come into being has educational needs different from those of yesterday's U.S. Dimly, we begin to define new educational goals, new paths, new attitudes. In the years when the U.S. was building a magnificent machine of mass education, pupils were regarded more or less as inert material to be processed toward testable standards of "achievement."

Now comes the dawning recognition that in an education system the main class of "decision makers" is, of all people, the students. Contemporary educational theory puts more stress on learning, less on teaching, as the main operational factor in the classroom. Students are no longer perceived as inert material to be manipulated toward goals clearly envisioned only by the educational hierarchy. Rather, education tends to be seen as a process in which pupils learn simultaneously to evolve both the goals and the means of pursuing them.

This way of looking at education obviously fits a nation in which individuality has become more important and the range of choice has greatly widened. But it does not fit the existing school system — a bureaucratically administered assembly line intended to produce a standardized product from undifferentiated materials.

Not surprisingly, the schools at the beginning of the Seventies were the target of widespread dissatisfaction. By the old norms, the schools seemed to be getting inadequate results for much higher per pupil expenditures. By the emerging norms, the schools seemed unresponsive to the needs of variety and individuality. In quest of flexibility and innovation, many parents support movements for neighborhood control, which would reverse a long trend toward administrative consolidation.

The lag between education and the general movement of the rest of American society has very grave implications, especially for politics. The high incidence of anti-authoritarian rebellion among the young may have its origin in the educational lag.

While business and almost every other segment of American life have limbered up, allowing more room for individual development and respecting it more, the schools cling to an older, tighter organizational model. It would be ironic and tragic if a substantial portion of the new generation of citizens had been conditioned by education to flail away at restraints that are not, in fact, characteristic of contemporary American life outside the schools.

It's not like pie or Scotch

Another increasingly urgent set of governmental problems relates to the physical environment. Some of the required government action in this field will take the familiar form of thou-shalt-not statutes. These will generate political disputes because one man's pleasure is another man's pollution. Our democratic processes, however, have handled many conflicts of this type and should be able to work toward better antipollution laws.

More difficult and more important will be the development of public policies intended to reshape the market structure of private decisions that affect the environment. How, for instance, can the social cost of dirty air and water be injected into the private accounts of producers and consumers? Graduated tax incentives and penalties provide one obvious answer, but the details of such policies will be very difficult to write and administer. We have not had much practice at that kind of government.

It is often said that the relative rise of spending by government, especially at the state and local levels, reflects a rising public demand for the services provided. That word "demand" is tricky. Nobody desires governmental services in the sense that he desires apple pie or Scotch. The citizen may be terribly hurt by the absence or interruption of services whose presence gives little joy.

Our complexifying society increases the need for these unenjoyable benefits. Resentment of taxes, of government, and of politics also increases, and can take such dangerous forms as rebellion, alienation, and apathy. The suburban dweller may be reluctantly willing to shoulder the burden of his own community's services, but he does not automatically perceive why he should pay a share of a central city's welfare or anticrime costs.

Only a few metropolitan areas have recently tried hard to solve these fundamental political problems in reconciling variety and unity, freedom and order. In Jacksonville, Florida, the black community, which had a prospect of controlling the city hall, was persuaded that it did not want to take over a bankrupt municipality. Simultaneously, suburban whites were persuaded that the short-run advantage of lower taxes was not worth the long-run danger of living in a metropolitan area with a decaying center. They consolidated city and suburban governments into a county-wide municipality.

The operational word in the above paragraph is "persuade." If citizens have civic needs that are not conscious desires, then governmental services have to be "sold" far more vigorously than they now are. The Columbia Broadcasting System attracted a lot of attention recently with a program called "The Selling of the Pentagon." Some public-relations pitches of the Defense Department are, indeed, open to criticism and rebuttal. But the implicit premise of the C.B.S. program that defense activities should not be "sold" to the public at all is nonsense. The boys aren't drilling with muskets on the village green anymore. Military activities, for which the public pays, would seem utterly incomprehensible unless there was a huge governmental effort to explain and justify them. Citizens don't have to "buy" the Pentagon's line. But every department of every level of government needs to do a lot more explaining and selling than was the case when governmental services were modest, simple, and self-evident.

There's a saying, "Justice must not only be done; it must be seen to be done." The point applies with mounting force to every function of government in a democratizing world. Foreign policy must not only be right; it must be seen to be right. Schools must not only be good; they must be seen (by the children) to be good. Policemen must not only be protectors of the people; they must be seen in that light.

In place of issues

All in all, the American political scene in the Seventies threatens to be highly fragmented and unstable. We are not likely to regain the political simplicity of clashes between pairs of very broad interest groups. The old regional structure of national politics has been weakening for decades. Broad class and ideological conflicts are diminishing. No single, continuing, transcendent issue is in sight.

Instead, the Seventies will see tens of thousands of political problems around which variant opinions, held with variant degrees of intensity, will transiently cluster. In that complex political framework, citizens will have to be far more attentive to government and to one another, and government will have to be more attentive to them.

The main line of political evolution in the Seventies will be the search for more appropriate ways of constituting the decision-making processes. It is in this literal sense that the next decade will be a time of "constitutional" politics. The Constitution of the United States probably will not need much, if any, amendment. It has been flexible enough to tolerate many governmental patterns and should be able to accommodate new ones — provided the nation still has the political energy and the civility that such changes require.

If in the Seventies the U.S. comes to understand the nature of its new governmental problems, if it begins to make visible headway in dealing with the challenge of expanding prosperity and freedom, then the present demoralization will be dispelled. Nothing would be better for the economy than a restored confidence that government can handle the political needs of the "new nation."